AMAZON F[...]

LEARN HOW TO SELL HIGH-PROFIT PRODUCTS WITH RETAIL ARBITRAGE. BUILD YOUR PRIVATE LABEL AND YOUR ECOMMERCE BUSINESS, CREATING A SUSTAINABLE PASSIVE INCOME STREAM IN 30 DAYS, OR LESS!

Benjamin Blue

© **Copyright 2019 - All rights reserved.**

The content contained within this book may not be reproduced, duplicated or transmitted without direct written permission from the author or the publisher.

Under no circumstances will any blame or legal responsibility be held against the publisher, or author, for any damages, reparation, or monetary loss due to the information contained within this book. Either directly or indirectly.

Legal Notice:

This book is copyright protected. This book is only for personal use. You cannot amend, distribute, sell, use, quote or paraphrase any part, or the content within this book, without the consent of the author or publisher.

Disclaimer Notice:

Please note the information contained within this document is for educational and entertainment purposes only. All effort has been executed to present accurate, up to date, and reliable, complete information. No warranties of any kind are declared or implied. Readers acknowledge that the author is not engaging in the rendering of legal, financial, medical or professional advice. The content within this book has been derived from various sources. Please consult a licensed professional before attempting any techniques outlined in this book.

By reading this document, the reader agrees that under no circumstances is the author responsible for any losses, direct or indirect, which are incurred as a result of the use of information contained within this document, including, but not limited to, — errors, omissions, or inaccuracies.

Table of Contents

Introduction 5

Choosing The Right Product 9

    Identifying Your Product Niche 10

    Discovering Trending and Profitable Products 13

    Validate Your Products through Hands-On Research 17

Finding Suppliers/Wholesalers For Your Business – Dealing With Distributers 19

How To Upgrade Your Living Status In A Month With Amazon FBA 29

    What You Need to Get Started out from Amazon 34

    Why Selling Online is Often Easier 38

How Fba Works 42

Mindset For Success 47

Amazon Tools For Getting Started 51

Advantages And Disadvantages To Amazon FBA 56

    Advantages 56

    Disadvantages 62

How To Sell Your Product? 68

How to Sell Like Crazy 80

    1. Introduction to Amazon Ads 80

    2. Unconventional Channels To Boost Your Sales 82

    3. SEO Strategies 83

4. Your Customers Are Your Best Friends 90
How To Create And Optimize The Perfect Product Page 93
    Branding Your Products on Amazon 93
    Advertising on Amazon 95
Pack It And Ship It 107
Filling The FBA Inventory 123
    Common Errors that Sellers make 129
Avoiding Common Mistakes 137
    Price Wars 138
    Shady Reviews 138
    Losing Money When Buying Overpriced Products 139
    Avoid the End of a Trend 141
    Not Taking Risks Is the Worst Mistake You Can Make 142
Conclusion 144

Introduction

These days, a lot of emphasis on being placed on the value of being able to work from home and earn money through your computer. For many, online marketing and e-commerce is a powerful opportunity to step out of financial ruin and into a state of financial freedom, with the added benefit of time freedom as well. With the way the economy seems to be going, I suspect that one day everyone will have some form of involvement in e-commerce as a way to subsidize or supplement their income, if not replace their income altogether.

You have likely seen the stories about people who decide to try e-commerce, only to realize that they tapped into a massive revenue stream that has earned those thousands, if not millions, of dollars every single year. From bloggers who have leveraged their websites for an income to individuals who have stepped onto platforms like Amazon, it seems like many have a form of "rags to riches" story that has left the rest of the world in awe. For many, it also seems like a deal that is simply too good to be true, and that they should not even bother trying because there is no way it could possibly work for them.

To those people, I say do your research.

E-commerce is a thriving powerhouse that continues to turn everyday people into individuals who are earning massive amounts of wealth and changing the future of their lives forever. There is no time like the present to get started, which is why I am so excited that you are here right now learning how to navigate the world of Amazon FBA!

Getting started as soon as possible is key in positioning yourself into the world of e-commerce and earning a piece of the pie for yourself. When you choose to get started with e-commerce, the moment you make the leap you set up the opportunity for your entire future to change. You not only open yourself up to create financial freedom for yourself, but you also set yourself up to receive many other benefits that come with financial freedom being earned through a strategy like e-commerce. For example, you create the opportunity for you to work from anywhere you desire, spend your days doing anything you wish to do, and design the lifestyle that you desire to have for yourself right down to the very last detail. Countless benefits come from the financial freedom and time freedom that you will earn for yourself through launching and managing a successful Amazon FBA business.

The best part is: this business can be built out in a highly passive manner, too. Many people think that you have to have a lot of time and energy to pour into launching an online business, or any business for that matter, in order to see it succeed. However, based on the nature of Amazon FBA and how this program works, you actually step into a form of e-commerce that is easier and more passive than virtually any other form of e-commerce out there. Through this platform, all you have to do is source products, place them for sale, and advertise them to your audience of individuals who are ready to purchase the products from you. Then, all you have to do is let Amazon employees manage the process of actually shipping your products to your customers, while you keep products in stock and source new products to grow your business with.

The concept of Amazon FBA is simple, which is exactly what makes it an incredible business opportunity for those who are new to e-commerce. Instead of having to manage everything from web development to inventory management, shipping and everything else, you simply have to manage marketing while making sure that everything stays in stock. This makes your role in the business wildly easy, meaning that you can grow your Amazon FBA business as a side business, or grow it and let the income sustain your freedom-based lifestyle.

In Amazon FBA, we are going to discuss everything you need to know about Amazon FBA, including what it is and how to get started with this business model. By the end of this book, you will be able to confidently design your own Amazon FBA business and grow it to massive success in minimal timing. Through this, you are going to be able to transform your own finances and open yourself up to the opportunity of living your best possible lifestyle.

If you are ready to begin learning the ways of Amazon FBA and preparing to launch your own Amazon FBA business, it is time to begin. Please, enjoy the process. You are about to make some massive, life-changing moves in the coming weeks!

Choosing The Right Product

Any retail business, including ones in the e-commerce industry, is only as strong as the products are. When it comes to generating success in your Amazon FBA business, you need to know how to choose the right products for you to sell to your customers so you can earn a strong profit and grow your business consistently over time. At this point, you have a clear understanding of the importance of identifying your competitive edge and you are already consciously and intentionally begun to develop this skillset. Now, you are going to use this understanding to find a product niche that works for you, and to find products that are going to work for your business.

When it comes to picking the right product niche and products for your business, it can be daunting as you realize the importance that this part of your business carries. You might fear that you will make the wrong decision and that you will struggle to generate any success in your business due to a poor choice made at this point. While this can certainly happen, there are plenty of strategies that you can use to help you calculate exactly what niche you should be selling in, and what products you should be selling as a part of that niche. Through using these calculations, you will be able to feel confident that the product niche and products that you choose are going to be profitable and popular enough to help you generate success. While nothing is guaranteed, if you follow these exact steps to verify and validate your product niche and products before committing in any one direction going forward, you will have the greatest odds in your favor.

Identifying Your Product Niche

Regarding identifying your product niche, you want to start by considering what industries you are most passionate about or interested in learning about. Many people underestimate the value of picking a niche that actually interests you, but true marketing masters know that this is the key to find a niche that you are going to be able to grow in. When you are passionate about, or at least interested in a certain subject, you are more likely to invest in learning about it and actually understand what it is that you are learning about. With marketing, this means that you are going to be far more intuitive about what types of trends are ideal for you to partake in, what products are going to succeed in your industry, and how you can grow your business effectively.

After you have identified about 3-5 passions or interests that you could pursue as a business venture, you want to start brainstorming all of the possible products and product lines that you could offer in each niche. Write those potential products or product lines down under each possible niche. In addition to writing down possible product lines, consider areas that you could branch out into as your business grew, too. For example, let us say you wanted to offer graphic t-shirts for women in a product line as your primary product line or the one that you would be starting in. Possible extensions of this could be to add male graphic t-shirts, child graphic t-shirts, and even graphic t-shirts for dogs. Alternatively, you could venture into offering graphic canvas bags, totes, and other female-oriented accessories if you wanted to maintain a female niche.

Getting a clear idea of what you could offer and how you could extend your offers is important, as this is your earliest opportunity to validate that your possible chosen niche would not only be strong in the beginning but would also have plenty of room for growth. Make sure that you take the time to really consider how these products would fit into your possible niche and whether or not they would make logical sense with your business. It is important that you are honest and concise when you validate possible product niches to feel confident that the route you have chosen is going to be a strong one. Now is not the time to be idealistic, but instead to be realistic, as you are going to be placing a lot of weight into this decision and you want to make sure that you minimize the risk as much as possible by validating it as honestly as possible right away.

Next, you need to start narrowing down your possible product niches into ones that are as specific as possible. While you do not want to niche down too hard to the point where you have almost nothing left to offer, you do want to niche down to the point where what you are offering is clear and easily groups together. For example, rather than saying "Gardening supplies" which is too broad or "gardening rakes" which is too specific, you might offer "designer flower pots" as a niche. This way, there are plenty of different product lines that you can incorporate, ranging from modern and sleek to flowery and feminine, yet it is still a clear niche that you are serving.

At this point, you can identify whether or not a niche is ideal based on your level of passion in that niche, the room for growth that it has, and the way that you might be able to narrow it down into a more specific category. All that is left to do is validate your niche with the outside world to ensure that the niche you pick is one that will actually interest other people, which will ensure that you are likely to earn sales from it. Nothing would be more disappointing than validating a niche with yourself, only to launch it to the public and find that it is something that not too many people are interested in.

When it comes to validating your niche, you can do so by researching your chosen niche on platforms like Google Trends. You can also do basic research on social media for your chosen niche by searching up hashtags or keywords relating to your niche and seeing just how popular those terms are. Ideally, you want a niche that has 2-5 million people interested in it so that you have plenty of room for growth. If there is any more than that, you might be attempting to tap into a niche that is far too broad for you to make any level of success. If you pick one that has a smaller audience, you are not going to have enough people to market to and you will find yourself marketing to no one.

At this point, since you are already researching, it is also a good idea to pay attention to the average price of products in your industry. Knowing this knowledge now will help you get an idea for what price points people are willing to buy the product at, which will help you determine if you are going to have a large enough profit margin to succeed with when you begin to source products for your business.

Discovering Trending and Profitable Products

Now that you have identified your niche, you need to start discovering products that you can sell in your niche that are going to sell quickly and earn you a strong profit along the way! With reference to selling products, there are a few things that you want to be on the lookout for as you choose which products to sell. These particular points are going to ensure that your product makes you the most money in the quickest period, making your business more successful.

When it comes to products that you will be selling online, you want to pick products that are trending, products that are easy to market, and products that are going to have a high-profit margin. You also want to pick products that are going to sell out quickly, as this means that you will not have to spend so much money on storage fees for the products that you are selling. The more that you can stock trending products that sell quickly, the more you are going to earn and the more momentum your store will grow with, which will result in you earning a huge income from your investment.

To begin identifying all of these highly profitable products, you want to start by doing some general product searches. General product searches involve you simply searching your niche on platforms like Amazon, Etsy, and eBay so that you can begin to see what types of products are most common in your chosen niche. Ideally, you want to look for products that retail between

$10 to $50, as these are the price points where impulse buys happen, which means that people are going to be likely to make quick purchases on your products. If you price any lower, people will not see it as being worth the investment, and if you invest it any higher people will need to think it over, which will mean it takes them longer to buy the products. In both cases, you are going to be waiting for sales, which will cost you more money and result in you having to work harder to make the sales.

As you do your general search, seek to write down 30-50 products that fall in this price range, including variables and alternatives that people are selling. The more products that you can note down, the better, as this will give you a strong list to pick through when you begin to decide what products you are actually going to sell in your store.

Next, you want to use a tool like Merchant Words or Jungle Scout, which is going to help you identify how strong the market is for products that you are planning on selling. These platforms help you see the exact analytics relating to supply and demand, ensuring that you are getting into a product where the supply exceeds the demand so that you can feel confident that you are going to have people to sell to. Items that are in demand are more likely to sell both at a higher volume, and at a higher speed, which results in you earning a higher profit and in a shorter period. This step should help you narrow your list down by knocking out any products that are not in high enough demand. Especially early on, you do not want to be investing in products that you are going to have to store for lengthy periods because you have chosen something that is not earning cash fast. Instead, you want to pick products that are likely to sell quickly so that you can build momentum and get your business out there, while also quickly earning back the investment that you put into your business.

With what is remaining on your list, you want to turn to Amazon's Best Seller Rankings and begin to identify whether or not your products are ranking well on Amazon itself. Ideally, you want to check out the first three to five products that are on Amazon's Best Seller Ranking's list to see which ones are going to be the most profitable for you in your niche. You can search for different categories that are related to your niche to get each of these products, which will help you validate all of the products that you have chosen to consider for your own business.

The last thing that you need to do when you are searching for products that you want to sell on Amazon FBA is looking at the actual FBA fees. Each type of product is going to have different fees due to it having a different shape, size, weight, storage requirement, and handling requirement than other products. Even products from the same niche will have different needs that will need to be accounted for in the fees, so always consider this before officially investing in the new product. This way, you can identify how much of your profits are going to be sunk into Amazon fees, which will help you determine whether it is worth it or not. For some products, the fees might eat up too much of your profit, leaving the product not worth it for you to truly invest in.

At this point, you should be left with a handful of products that are going to be ideal for you to sell in your store. Do not worry about how many you have identified to sell unless you have had a hard time finding good products as this may indicate that you have picked too specific of a niche or one that is not strong enough for you to sell in. However, if you find that you have 20-45 products or more on a list of possible purchases, this is a good thing. This proves that there is a strong variety of great products for you to sell and that you will have plenty to grow out into later on.

Validate Your Products through Hands-On Research

Just like with your product niche, you are also going to need to validate your products through actual humans. Understand that just because your niche and product popularity prove positive does not mean that you are going to know how to immediately access the people who are going to be most likely to buy your product. If you are not tapping directly into those consumers, you are going to have a hard time getting people to buy from you.

Validating your products through hands-on research allows you to get a feel for where your possible consumers are spending time online and how you can get ahold of them. This way, if you do begin selling that particular product you know exactly where to go to market your product and earn as many sales as possible right off the bat.

The best way to begin validating your audience is by going onto social media platforms and looking up your particular niche on social media. Better yet, search keywords related to your chosen product and get a feel for how many people are talking about that product or using that product in their everyday lives. Ideally, you should see hundreds of thousands of people using those products on each platform that you choose to visit to prove that there is a strong audience for you to market to right away.

As you validate your products this way, make sure that you take note of which keywords and hashtags are turning you up with the best results for where you can find your audience online. Although keeping notes on this information will not be relevant to you right now, it will help you later on when it comes time to market your products, as you will already know where to look to find the people who are most likely to buy them. When you are ready to step into your launch, already having part of the research completed will make the launch process easier for you to do.

Finding Suppliers/Wholesalers For Your Business – Dealing With Distributers

Finding the right supplier or the right wholesalers for your Amazon FBA business is imperative, meaning that you can't "cheap out" or not care about this aspect. As you can imagine, your business will revolve around your supplier quite heavily. Truth be told, if you don't have any products that you can sell, then it would honestly be impossible for you to make any money which would, therefore, equal no profits. On the other hand, if you decide to "cheap out" and sell low-quality products, chances are people will return the products.

Finding the right supplier for your Amazon FBA business purposes is imperative for both quality purposes and shipping purposes. Now, if you are going to be using Amazon FBA or a similar type of Amazon FBA method, then shipping times do matter in order for you to stock up your products, but it isn't the biggest of the deal for that Amazon FBA model when compared to Amazon FBA methods using Shopify. Now with all that said, quality is the biggest factor you have to worry about when selling your products. So today, we will go through the top websites from where you can find great suppliers for your business. We will also talk about how to build a great relationship with them, and finally, for everyone using the dropshipping method online, I will reveal a secret to get the fastest shipping anywhere in the world so your customers stay happy and fewer refunds are being made.

We will break this chapter into two phases. First, we will talk about how to find suppliers for people using online Amazon FBA. We will go through everything from finding the product, to building a relationship with the seller, getting it shipped fast, and of course, making sure the product is of high quality. Then we will talk about finding a supplier or a whole-seller for the warehouse method.

Online Amazon FBA

So, finding a supplier for people using online Amazon FBA as their business model could be challenging. Since most of the time you will be going by assumptions, your job is to take out as much of the guesswork as we can and find the winning supplier. Now, there are a lot of websites online where you can find products for cheap. But from my experience, AliExpress has some of the best quality products and shipping times. If you have been doing some research online, you might have heard things like "AliExpress is dead" or things of that nature. But I am here to tell you that AliExpress still works amazingly and will help you make some serious profits online. There are some tips and techniques you need to know before you fully start using AliExpress as your sole supplier.

Now, if you don't know what Ali Express is, then let me clarify it for you. Think of AliExpress as the Amazon of China. There are a lot of people selling products online on this website, mostly from China. As we know, most of the products are manufactured in China, meaning the mark upon the products will be a lot less. You can easily sell these products online for a higher price in the North American market. To make things even better, the products on AliExpress are mostly similar types of products that are sold or are popular in the North American market. The point I am trying to make is this; people selling on Ali Express are selling especially to people who want to start their Amazon FBA business.

There are some guidelines you need to follow before you start to use AliExpress to drop-ship products from, as there are some flaws. The things we need to look into before we start selling products using Ali Express are:

- Suppliers reviews
- Product photos and description
- E-packet
- How many orders sold

Now, if all of these points are checked out and prove good, then your supplier is good. So, let's begin with the supplier review. To find out if the supplier is good, the first thing you will need to do is check the reviews. Make sure the review on his or her store is at least 95% positive. If that's not the case, then either the quality of the product isn't good or the product is something else when it gets delivered. Another thing to worry about is photos and the description. If the product has great photos and descriptions, then most of the time it shows that the seller actually cares about what he or she is doing and will do whatever it takes to keep his customers happy.

Another thing to take care of is shipping. If the seller offers a shipping method known as e-packet, then the shipping times will be a lot faster than other suppliers. Normally, e-packet delivers the product in 2-3 weeks, which is the fastest shipping time you will get on Ali Express, so make sure your supplier provides you with e-packet. Also, to make sure this supplier is reliable, check out how many orders he/she has had. If it is higher than 500 orders then they are in the clear. If all the points I just described to you checked out well, then the supplier is good and you can truly start to grow your business with him or her. And if the supplier doesn't check out on all these points, then find a new one.

One more tip I would share with you; Ali Express tends to take some time when processing a payment. It could take up to three days. It is done simply for their security. If you want to expedite the process of payment for your order to be shipped even faster, then I would recommend using Ali pocket. Ali pocket is similar to a gift card. It is like a safe credit card for Ali Express, so if you buy Ali pocket in bulk and use it to buy the product which you will be shipping out to your client, no time will be wasted processing payments and the order would be shipped right away.

Now, AliExpress is great for selling new trending stuff. But if your goal is to sell fan t-shirts and things of that nature, then it might not be the right choice for you.

AliExpress has a lot of things to sell online, but the products it sells are not specific to niches and people. This is where print-on-demand t-shirts come in.

What is print-on-demand, you might ask? Well, print-on-demand is a service where you come up with a logo. Pick out a plain t-shirt sweater or whatever they have, then the company will use your logo and put it on a t-shirt, etc. and directly ship it out to the customer or the buyer. That is what print-on-demand is. Now, there are a lot of websites to choose from. But the one I highly recommend is Pillow Profits. It is amazing - not only do they have your good old t-shirts, but they also offer things like pillowcases, shower curtains or bedsheets which can be sent to a customer with your logo on any of those things.

Now print-on-demand is ideal for those super niche fan pages we talked about before. Since those fan pages are unique and hard to find, you need to be really unique with your products just like the pages you are promoting it to. So, if your store is based on super-niche products, then it would be hard to find products on Ali Express and this is where print-on-demand comes in.

Most of the print-on-demand websites have a really fast delivery since most of them are based in areas out of the United States. So, you don't need to worry about shipping or any of that. Just make sure to pick out a print-on-demand website you like and come up with a logo.

Let's talk about building relationships with your suppliers. It is imperative that you build a great relationship with your supplier. Not only will it help you make more profits, but it will also help you get faster shipping times. What I am about to tell you applies more to AliExpress rather than print-on-demand websites. Regardless of which website it is, you need a great relationship with your supplier. So, in order to build great relationships with your suppliers, here are the ways you can do so.

- Give them business
- Be accepting
- Leave them great reviews

Giving them business is quite self-explanatory. If you want to build a great relationship, you have to give them business.

You can't expect to be their "special customer" if you don't buy anything from them. So, make sure you first buy at least 20-25 items before you can think about asking them for a discount on your products. Another thing to be mindful of is making sure you don't get angry at them for a shipment which is a couple of days late or things of that nature. You have to remember that they are trying their best to keep you happy, just like you are trying to keep your customers happy. So, make sure you are accepting and not making a big deal about small things like these. The final thing is to leave a positive review because let's face it, everyone cares about positive reviews. If you follow all these steps, you will start to build a great relationship with your supplier and you can slowly start to ask for things like discounts on your orders which would mean higher profit margins for you. So, make sure you start to build a great relationship with them.

With all that said, that is all for finding a supplier for people using online Amazon FBA. Let's talk about finding suppliers for people using Amazon FBA or warehouse Amazon FBA. It is a little bit different but shares some of the same principles.

Warehouse Amazon FBA

To find suppliers or products for this type of Amazon FBA is a little bit easier when compared with online Amazon FBA. Since you can inspect all the products before you start selling, it makes it one step easier. So, in short, there are three ways you can go about finding a supplier. The first one is using sites like AliExpress. The second one is to find a warehouse where they are selling the products for cheap, and finally, buying products in special sales and reselling them.

Now, you already know how to find the right supplier on AliExpress, but let's talk about how you can use AliExpress for warehouse Amazon FBA. So, right off the bat, once you find a product that you would like to sell, I would highly recommend you buy one of the products and really check its quality. Once you have checked it out and made sure that the quality is of a high caliber, then you should contact the supplier and work out a deal. You see, since you will be buying the product in bulk, there will be higher chances of you getting it for a further discounted price, so make sure you ask for it so you can make even more profit. Finally, once that is all done, ship it to the warehouse and start selling.

That was using AliExpress. Now, let's talk about using warehouses or special sales to find your supplies. People don't realize that there are a lot of warehouses like Costco where you can buy stuff for cheap and sell it on Amazon. The way this process works is simple. Go to a warehouse such as Costco, find a product in bulk for really cheap, and then transport it to Amazon's warehouse and start selling. Trust me, I have found so many cheap products in Costco for sale which have made me some great profits! Make sure you find these products and start selling them on Amazon.

Finally, one of the ways I have made tremendous amounts of money on Amazon FBA is by waiting for sales like Black Friday and things of that nature. I would buy products on sale for 50% to even 70% off and after the sale is done, I would sell it on Amazon at its original price. Although this method is not as frequently occurring as the other two, it will yield you a lot of profits so make sure you wait for these sales to make some real cash.

Finally, one secret method I have used before is finding listings on Craigslist and Facebook marketplaces for products and supplies. Most of the time, you will find brand new stuff for sale near you, and the seller will be selling it off for next to nothing. So, this would be your time to shine. Find something in bulk for really cheap on these websites. Work out a deal and sell it off on Amazon for a great profit. Now if you found something cheap but the quantity is low, then I would recommend using eBay to sell it on. I remember finding a brand new iPhone for super cheap, so just like anyone else, I bought it and sold it off on eBay for a great profit. So, whatever you can find on these websites for cheap, make sure to act on them as soon as possible before they are gone.

To conclude this chapter, I would just like to remind you how important it is to have the right supplier. A great supplier can either make your business or break it. Making sure you have the right supplier is imperative as it will help you have a longer sustained business. So please, make sure you read this chapter very carefully and practice all the tricks and techniques taught in this chapter in order for you to find the right supplier. Don't settle for a product or supplier which "gets the job done." If you want your business to be the best it can be, then find a product or supplier which is the best you can find in terms of service quality, and of course, the price. But also, don't forget to keep your suppliers happy. Like I said, if you want better deals on your products, you need to make sure your relationship with your supplier is great.

How To Upgrade Your Living Status In A Month With Amazon FBA

Amazon FBA (Fulfilment by Amazon) is an incentive given to business owners by Amazon to list their goods in their market.

The model works by Amazon and allows users to send their products to their warehouse, which the retained giant "completes" (sends them) after successful purchases.

This would be partly because Amazon gets free niche products that are exclusive and desirable (you own the products, they're just delivering them for you), and partly to make use of their huge infrastructure (they'd pay anyway).

It also adds to their offer as a company, as a range of products to add to their portfolio (which is almost their core competitive advantage).

The important thing about the "FBA" model is that it represents the current "digital" business culture that seems to have become more popular after the 2008 crash. Instead of holding big stock, overheads, and a big team… Companies have used the Internet and social media to find buyers and create lean companies.

The days are gone when distributors have determined the destiny of products. Today, new companies, entrepreneurs, and everyday citizens can produce $10,000+ a month's income without having to own property. The entire infrastructure, marketing, and legislation are handled by an independent company (Amazon), which only exists to achieve a successful product.

To order to find out whether you want to benefit from this investment strategy, I have developed this guide to show you the process of using Amazon FBA. Instead of trying to get through the scraps from a local market, a modern "digital" domain with its promise is one of the best ways to get your foot in the new world.

Both companies are working in the same way-buy / create a product, sell the product for the market, and any "benefit," which you can produce, can be used either to live off or to reinvest in more / better products.

For most people, the issue is double: 1) they don't have a commodity, 2) they don't have market access.

Whereas both issues are real-that would have been a major drawback in a period without the "digital" media-times have gone so far that barriers to entry are so small that you need to spend just $1,000 to market them to a global audience.

And while the "Amazon" has been around for nearly ten years (anyone can list products on their market), the "FBA" model (truly hand-off) has only begun to be very popular in the past 24 months or so.

If you have not attended business school to illustrate briefly how to run a successful organization, you need to be in a position to deliver a product/service to a wide audience. You would typically aim for a net profit margin of about 30 percent (after COGS & advertising costs). How you do this is up to you - it is important that you buy low, sell high.

Now it doesn't mean that the "digital" realm is large without how "markets" usually work. Competition obviously is a major force, as is the idea that, because something is "easy," it can be quite simply replicated by others (which leads to your profit erosion).

Amazon sales typically work by providing access to products that people either do not buy locally or can purchase locally but with significant limitations (such as color/size issues) or problems with supply reliability. In other words, while the competition in Amazon is huge-don't believe you can overcome supply/demand.

The real task for "digital" businesses is to offer access to unique products (usually made by yourself or your company) that are only available through you. Such goods must be aimed at providing a solution that most people do not know and therefore make the offer to purchase it via the Internet valid.

Obviously, it is 1000 times easier than done to create a "unique" product, and the trick is to work on solutions to your problems. Work to sharpen a knowledge set that can be applied to a broader public, which will enable you to identify "products" that can be created and offered as a means of simplifying/solving yourself problems.

Steps to start selling on Amazon, you have to do several things: sign up for the Amazon seller account. Two kinds of seller account are available-" individual "and" professional. Individuals are free and encourage you to "check" products that are already in the Amazon catalog. Every time a product is sold, you pay a small fee. Professional costs $40/m, without any additional "per sale" fees (although other fees can apply, such as storage fee, etc.). This is the only account you can list in the Amazon catalog.

Subscribe to GS1. It helps you to create* barcodes *. They are available in two formats: Universal Product Code (UPC) and European Article Number (EAN). Although these can be purchased relatively cheaply ($10), GS1 for standardization is strongly recommended by Amazon, Google, and eBay. By using GS1, you can recognize your products like Amazon. The bottom line is the cost, but it really shouldn't matter—we still suggest setting~$500 apart for administrative costs.

Create a legal corporation (optional) You'll need a legal business (and bank accounts) if you want to set up a real FBA operation. In addition to allowing Amazon to open a business account, it also helps you to handle taxes better (which are notoriously bad when spending your personal money). This is very simple to set up, but only if you really want to work with Amazon on an FBA basis. You are welcome to do so under your own name if you only want to sell products on the network.

You then have to get a set of boxed versions of the drug. You will put the goods into uniform boxes if you design them yourself. Because there are so many ways, we're just going to tell you to look for a boxing/printing company to deal with it for you. There are many that are capable. You also have to follow the guidelines of Amazon on what packaging forms they support.

Once you have the goods shipped, you have to give them to Amazon. The Amazon selling system allows you to choose a time when the products should be delivered in the Amazon warehouse. However, because of the variation in the process, it is better to say that to do so, you will obey the Amazon guidelines.

Products sales The last move is to sell the products. This is the worst, as you are virtually entirely at the mercy of the consumer (Amazon and every other company that you can add to the platform).

Good marketing is the secret to getting goods from Amazon.

Marketing is based on several factors–the notable thing is that you need first to attract the attention of potential purchasers and then create demand—to give them the chance to purchase the product as a way to meet this demand.

While there are many ways to do that, you have to bear in mind that if you do it successfully, you must be able to market the product irrespective of whether it is popular on Amazon. The less you need Amazon, the more likely you get people to buy via the web.

Ultimately, we must not be considered as pure profit for any sales you make.

Your benefit only comes after your other expenses (such as your own goods, boxes, and marketing) have been compensated for. It's a big mistake to think the money you get from Amazon is your "take-home" benefit-not.

What You Need to Get Started out from Amazon

It's easy to start selling at the Amazon market. You probably have most of these things already on hand. If the money is tight, buy small quantities (envelopes, tape, and bubble wrap for shipping) to save during your startup process. You can buy in bulk later and save money. You will need: a computer with Internet access-you already have your computer when you are reading this. You need to check book prices every day, list books for sale, and email updates.

Shipment envelopes— Tall 9"x 12" and 10"x 13" brown manila envelopes fit very well to ship the bulk of the books.

Bubble wrap-Protect books against email damage. You can buy a light bubble roll in many discount stores for about $5 to start these days. It saves you money against buying envelopes from bubble wrap and helps you to ship items on eBay or other websites with online sellers.

USPS Confirmation Slips-These is available free of charge from your local post office. It's the green and white slips which have one end of a peel-and-stick glue. Request a 50-100 stack to get started.

Black ink pens–plenty have to manage orders, confirmation of delivery slips, dispatch labels, and note-making.

Eraser Pencils–many libraries and some thrift shops will be able to mark the internal front cover with a pencil price before it is sold. This price is usually $1, $2, $3–and you will need to clear that you got an awesome bargain when you sell it ten times as much as you paid for it!

Scissors-To trims poorly wrapped boxes and cut down protective cardboard packaging to carry small booklets or containers. You will also need them to cut the bubble wrap that you will use to ship books.

File folders-Use some old manila folders you'd get rid of if you don't want to buy new ones for a small package, which costs around $5. Trim them into two parts, one to protect your book front and the other to protect the book's back cover, until you slip your book into the shipping envelope to give your package extra security.

Clear heavy- tape pistol & duty shipping tape-You'll need to start with a tape gun and 2-3 clear tape rolls. If you have short cash, you could purchase the smaller plastic band dispensers for around $3 each.

Cleaning supplies— These are probably in your kitchen already: towels of paper, tiny clean brush, warm water. to avoid stains, using not cleaning sprays or dust covers from books. Most of the time, you can put a little warm water on the paper towel, spray it across glittering dust covers and restore a clean shine to the book cover.

Bookshelves-Of course, these business inventories tend to take up lots of space, so put aside an extra bedroom or a cool, dry spot in your low-moisture home, away from windows which sweat in order to prevent paper damage from the books, and invest in or create a shelf for your books.

Work Table-Yes, but a dedicated work table, which can be placed in a utility cabinet, is a good way of getting an assembly line going to (1) listing books and (2) preparing books for shipping.

Mobile smartphone-Okay, I'm going to admit this is optional. Many mobile phones take a big piece of your monthly budget. But when you use the web browser of the phone when you shop, you know, for sure, if you have found a winner in seconds, so that there's no second-guessing.

Set-Up Account-You will need a company checking account to deposit direct payments into your book sales. Ask your bank for a free debit card, and you will not have to write many checks from this account. You can use the debit card to buy the books that you need to start and operate. You'll need a credit card– you'll need one for Amazon to confirm your seller's account on the day you startup (it isn't charged after that).

You'll have to have a telephone number-a home name or a cell phone number that Amazon will use to send to you when you set up an account, a confirmation call or a text message confirming your identity (this is a telephone number that will not be published in your online shop unless you want to put it there - and I recommend against.

Check with your city zoning department–I'm not aware that some cities are limiting home business. You may need a commercial license in your city. You will not have customers and suppliers who sell you, and unless you have UPS collect large volumes of your books to the nearest distribution center "Fulfilled By Amazon" (FBA), your neighbors are likely never to notice that you are operating a domestic business unless you tell them about it.

Now that you know the essential items to start selling Amazon used books, it's time to make busy selling books online. If you store the right kind of books, it's easy to make money. Take time, negotiate the best deals, and restrict your purchases to good books. Your home-based book store takes time to get up and running, but having the right tools to start handy can help you get to more in less time as you know how to sell at Amazon!

Why Selling Online is Often Easier

The definition of what selling is all about in the dictionary is simple and straightforward and covers most of your knowledge about the physical action of selling. However, this ignores the psychology of sales, to which we will return in this report on several occasions.

Nonetheless, if we embrace this basic definition, for now, we can start examining the similarities between internet sales and the real-world marketing of highway, brick, and mortar firms.

The main difference between online sales and real-world sales is that your whole internet sales process is far less personal than you would if you sell products or services to local businesses in your area.

Imagine, for example, being a salesman for a local offline business. Here, you would constantly call existing customers and prospects, make appointments to visit them, sort out your customers' issues, and so on. Simply put, it would be realistic because while you would not do something face-to-face, a large proportion of your day-to-day job would include meeting clients and experiences in person.

As one with over 25 years of experience working with sales teams that have sold a wide range of real-world products and services (from long term investment plans to toner cartridges for laser printers), for most people who do not think they can sell, it is the most expensive and stressful thing to meet customers or prospects face to the side. This is perfectly natural because you are most exposed and' naked' at a face-to-face meeting of this nature. You are in a position where you feel uncomfortable and maybe embarrassed, a position where mistakes are most frequently made.

For example, many young vendors were too eager to please prospects and customers who fell in the trap of making very basic mistakes in their understandable desire to keep their customers (and boss) happy.

One classic situation is that, when you have a question you do not know the answer, you make (at best) a rather uneducated guess about what you think might be the correct answer. Instead of doing the right thing, you tell the customer that you do not know the answer but are going back to the office to find the information before returning to the customer.

The latter ' study and report ' approach is natural and comfortable when experience shows you that you never can know all about your business and what your clients do not really expect you either. But in the early days, it's a different story because new salesmen often find it hard to admit that they don't know all.

Then contrast this scenario with the situation of online sales. If you promote a product or service online, you rarely speak to a client over the telephone and reach them much less. This does not mean you cannot do this, of course, and there may be benefits, as we will see.

However, the majority of online marketers will always have only a small amount of personal interaction with their customers and clients, partly because of the truly global nature of online businesses and partly because it is not really anticipated. Moreover, any personal contact which exists is unlikely to require an immediate answer to inquiries or questions "on-the-spot," so there is much less pressure.

Since most communication between online companies and customers or prospects is likely to occur via email, or short messages to back and forth through messaging services, such as Skype, Yahoo or MSN, it is much less possible for you to make any mistakes by trying to provide immediate information as it is in the business world offline. In other words, there is considerably less pressure.

Today, it doesn't have to be said that the online business world is perfect because this lack of personal communication and interaction will create its own problems. When, for example, you are dealing with a client or prospect face-to-face, you will be able to read the language of their bodies and focus on their responses to what you are doing. When you communicate with someone via email, you obviously cannot "sense" what your prospects or customers really need or want in their language.

Consequently, the capacity for confusion and even disagreements has increased slightly. This is one of the reasons why the use of humor in this type of situation is often a bad idea because humor doesn't usually transcend international borders very well and what you think is amusing could seem ironic or disinfectant to anyone else.

How Fba Works

Understanding FBA and its functioning is really easy. All you have to do is send your inventory to an Amazon Fulfillment Center, and from there on the Amazon people take care of it. They'll handle all the back-end operations. They do everything from storing inventory to fulfilling orders to handling customer support and order returns. They're very consistent about it, which improves your reliability as a seller. It's totally up to you how much you want to store, according to your finances.

Here's how you register for FBA:

1)   Open the following URL on your web browser: amazon/fba.

2)   Click on "Get Started."

3)   You don't have to register for a Seller Central account since you already have one. You just have to select "Add FBA to your account".

4)   Then log in to your Seller Central account and check the Inventory tab.

5)   Click on the "Manage Inventory" option and choose which products you would like to list for FBA. There's a checkbox next to each product and you can mark it to list it for FBA.

6) Once you've selected all the products you want to list, click on the Actions drop-down menu, and select "Change to Fulfilled by Amazon."

7) On the next page, click on "Convert."

After this, you have to ready your stock and send it to an Amazon Fulfillment Center. Here are the instructions for doing that:

1) Go to your account's Inventory tab.

2) Click on "Manage Inventory" and once again, mark the checkboxes against the items you want to go for FBA.

3) Then click on the Actions drop-down menu, and select "Send/Replenish Inventory."

4) Then you'll be asked to give a shipping address. Provide the necessary details.

5) You will be asked how you're going to ship the products: case-packed or individual items.

Note: Before you do this, make sure to take a look at the Dangerous Units, Hazardous Materials, and EBA Prohibited Products page, to be sure everything is legal.

The next step is to review the labeling requirements. Amazon's receiving systems are dependent on barcodes; so all units you send to them must be tagged with a barcode that is able to be scanned. There are three ways to do this:

1) Manually print and apply labels to each unit.

2) Use the Label Service from FBA itself. Everything will be handled by Amazon.

3) If your products are eligible, sign up for the Stickerless Commingled Inventory.

Here are Amazon's recommendations for when you are preparing to print labels for your products:

•Use a laser or a thermal printer and avoid inkjet printers. This will decrease the chances of fading and smearing.

•Your printer should be able to handle resolutions above 300DPI.

•Make sure you're using the right print media.

•Regularly clean and replace your printer heads.

•Test your labels periodically by scanning them yourself. See if they're legible.

You will receive a PDF file once you have entered the number of units you'll be shipping for each product. You can print these labels later. Again, there are some guidelines:

•Use white-label stock with removable adhesive to print the labels. This makes them easily scannable and removable.

•Make sure only the product label that Amazon provided is visible. If there are other barcodes on your product/package, hide them all properly.

•Some products require prepping before they are shipped, which can slow down the shipping process. To avoid this, you can use FBA Prep Services. You can also send them fully prepped to the fulfillment centers.

•Each box sent to Amazon should have a unique shipping label. It's the only way to identify it at the fulfillment center.

Here are your guidelines for attaching the labels:

•Don't place the labels on a place where they'll be cut. Try to place them in the middle of the box if possible. Never place them on the seams or corners.

•There must be a unique shipping label on each box.

•If there are pallets, each one has to have five labels. One goes on the top and the others go on each side.

When all of this is done, schedule a time for the pickup of your inventory. Mark all the items you are shipping as "Shipped" in the Shipment Summary. From there on, you can track the status of your shipment in the Shipping Queue. Allow a period of at least 24 hours before checking whether the status is updated to "Delivered." After that, you can contact your carrier to confirm delivery.

"Checked-In" means that some part of your shipment has reached, and they're waiting for the rest. Once the barcode scanning starts; the status again changes to "Receiving." The whole process usually takes about six days, so be patient. After this, the dimensions of all your products are recorded. Once they're stored, they can be shipped anytime.

Amazon's web-to-warehouse picking system is very advanced. It can sort through inventories in the warehouse really fast and when a customer purchases something, it will pick the right method of shipping them the product according to their preference. The order can be accurately tracked by the customer throughout the shipping process. This makes for a very pleasant experience for the customer.

Mindset For Success

How to Have the Right Mindset

We will talk about what you should be doing to make sure that you are not failing in your endeavors to start this Amazon FBA to live a healthier life overall. This chapter will show you what you could be doing to make this Amazon FBA your lifestyle and to not only help you to start the Amazon FBA and stay on track, but also to live with this plan for the rest of your life. These daily patterns will help you to not fail with your Amazon FBA. We understand that you may fail a couple of times in any Amazon FBA, and it is understandable to do so. Nonetheless, this chapter will show you how to make sure you are consistent and not failing. These habits have been followed by many successful people to get optimal results in all of their aspects of life, whether it is fitness related or anything else. Make sure you start implementing all these habits after you are done reading this book as it will help you to make this Amazon FBA your lifestyle. The reason why this chapter might sound philosophical is that the only way you will see success with this Amazon FBA is if you do it consistently. For you to do that, you need to change your current lifestyle by being more productive and disciplined. You have to remember that healthy eating is for more than just an Amazon FBA; it's a lifestyle.

Plan your day ahead

Planning your day ahead of time is crucial, Not only does planning out your day help you be more prepared for your day moving forward, but it will also help you to become more aware of the things you shouldn't be doing, hence That are wasting your time.

Moreover, planning your day will truly help you with making the most out of your time. That being said, we will talk about two things:

- Benefits of planning out your day
- How to go about planning out your day

So, without further ado, let us dive into the benefits of planning out your day.

It will help you prioritize

Yes, planning out your day will help you prioritize a lot of things in your day-to-day life. You can allocate time limits to the things you want to work on the most to least, for example, if you're going to write your book and you are super serious about it. Then you need a specific time limit every day in which you work on a task wholeheartedly without any worries of other things until the time is up. Then you move on to the next job in line, so when you schedule out your whole day and you give yourself time limits, then you can prioritize your entire day.

The same thing goes for your Amazon FBA, make sure you allocate time for prepping your plans for the next day, which will allow you to have goals ready for you when you need it, hence making it easy for you to continue with your Amazon FBA.

More focus on the task on hand

With the time limit on all tasks that you do daily, it will create an urgency to get as much of the job done as you can before time is up and you are moving on to your next appointment, which will help you be more focused on the task at hand and get more things done. Many people consider planning your day out to be time-consuming, which it isn't if you prioritize your time the right way. If you plan your goals the day before, then it should not be a problem.

Work-Life Balance

You see, once you start planning out your whole day, you become more aware of your time and how to balance it out. Once you begin to write out your entire day ahead of you, you will know precisely what you are doing that day so you don't have to do anything sporadically throughout the day. Always plan some time for yourself every day where you can wind down, read a good book, meditate, or maybe hang out with your friends. You will feel refreshed the next day. Having to wind down and "chill out" will only make you a more productive person.

Planning out your whole day ahead will not only help you prioritize better. It will also help you be more focused on your task on hand and will help you have a better work-life balance. This will help you to stay motivated with the Amazon FBA that you are following. So now that we have discovered the benefits of planning out your day, let's dive into the how-to's when it comes to planning out your day.

Summarize your Normal Day

Now, before we start getting into planning out your whole day, you need to realize that to plan your entire day, you need to know precisely what you are doing that day. This means you need to write down every single thing you do on a typical day and write down the time you start and end. It needs to be detailed in terms of how long it takes for your transportation to get to work, etc.

Now after you have figured out your whole day, you can decide how to prioritize your day. It could be cutting out a task that you don't require or shortening your time for a job that doesn't need that much time. After you have your priorities for the day, you can add pleasurable tasks into your day like hanging out with your friends, etc.

Amazon Tools For Getting Started

There are many tools that you will need to get started with selling on Amazon. In this chapter, you will find a list of essential tools that will help you in starting out as a seller on Amazon.

Freightos:

Every part of the selling machinery on Amazon is automated, except the part where a salesperson will have to import their goods to the Amazon warehouse(s). Dealing and coordinating with freight movers can be a time-consuming process, and you will never know if you are getting a good deal or not. Freightos offers an international freight calculator, letting you compare the freight prices of air, water and trucking costs in an instant. Not just that, but you can also compare the prices of different logistics providers as well. This will help to ensure that you are getting the best available price on your freight charges.

Sellics:

Everything that you will require to start selling on Amazon is made available in one place with Sellics. There are seven different features that this tool offers. The most attractive features offered by it include keyword ranking, inventory management, and profit calculation. You can categorize and analyze the benefits at the SKU level as well as by organic or PPC sales. Profit calculation is quite detailed, and it includes several filters like the cost of goods sold, costs of inbound shipping, and much more.

JoeLister:

This is perhaps the quickest way an Amazon seller can list their inventory—not just on Amazon, but on eBay as well. It will save you lots of time and effort by creating an inventory listing for Amazon. It only takes a few clicks, and this application will make sure that your item quantities are synced so that you don't oversell. Whenever a sale is made, this application will create a multi-channel fulfillment order on Amazon along with the tracking information. And you, as a seller, won't have to do anything. It will also help you to make decisions regarding pricing and help the buyers leave an automatic feedback as well. What's more? You can take advantage of this service for free for two weeks. If you feel that it will be beneficial, then you can subscribe to it.

Forward2me:

This application provides a service for managing returns, and it offers two essential services. It provides customer returns and the return of excess stock. According to Amazon guidelines, sellers will have to provide a local address for receiving the returns, or they have to pay for return orders or return shipping on all the returns. For a retailer selling from a foreign location, this can be an expensive process. This application provides a very simple solution to manage this issue and reduce the overall costs. You can also make use of this application to make sure that the excess stock or inventory is returned from Amazon's warehouse to your location. You need to provide Forward2me with your forwarding address, and this application will do the rest. The sign-up process is quite simple as well.

Amazon Seller App:

If you are interested in retail arbitrage, then this is a great application for scanning products that you have come across and you think might have the potential to be sold on Amazon FBA. What's more? This application is free of cost. You can try out Amazon FBA without spending too much on acquiring inventory. It also allows a seller to list particular items available for sale, contact Amazon, and respond to customer inquiries. It allows you to check the current rates, sales ranking, and customer feedback by using the text-based search option.

Inventory Lab:

Inventory Lab, as the name suggests, allows a seller to manage not just their inventory but their accounting as well. This application allows sellers to check their profitability and keep an inventory of their stock in real-time. You can even print labels directly through this application. The elegant yet robust accounting provisions of this application will help you keep track of all your business expenditures.

Scoutify:

Inventory Lab developed this app, and it allows sellers to explore multiple competitive deals on Amazon through their phones. The user interface is very easy, and it offers a lot of helpful features. This application comes with Bluetooth scanner compatibility; a seller can see the gross profit of each product, weigh in the costs for the calculation of net profit, review their search history and monitor any decline in earnings, estimate the taxes to be paid, and so on.

Camelcamelcamel:

If you want to consider FBA as a seller, then this is one of the most useful tools available, and it is free. This helps to monitor the price listings of products on Amazon, keeps track of the sales, and much more. This application includes a browser add-on, provides you with Amazon's price charts, and also tracks the price changes as well. This application enables you to set up alerts for price and availability, whenever there are any changes. Prices of listings will constantly be updated from Amazon to make the data as reliable as possible.

Profit Bandit:

This isn't a free application, but the price you pay for it is quite reasonable. It offers services like a built-in filter that automatically shows the profit or loss of individual products. It also has the option to display collectibles, and you are allowed to research within this platform before deciding on your sales by checking other websites.

Price Blink:

This application is a software add-on, and it provides you with details about items that are offered for a lower price on other websites. If you are looking to sell a particular product through Amazon, then you can make use of this application to check if the same is being offered for a lower price on other websites. This comes in handy if you are leaning towards retail arbitrage. This platform can be easily accessed and is quite unobtrusive. When you click on a particular listing on this portal, it will check the web and show you the results. You can compare the prices and price your products accordingly.

Advantages And Disadvantages To Amazon FBA

Just as with any other company, Amazon FBA has many advantages and disadvantages. Be informed about your decision to set up a business with Amazon FBA by being aware of how each part of the company can affect your business.

Most businesses use Amazon FBA in conjunction with their own websites, and this is often because the business and exposure they get from Amazon FBA translates into their outside businesses. It is wise to have a stake in both a personal website and Amazon FBA account, though we will not go into further detail here. Suffice it to say that, before you fully commit yourself to sell on Amazon full-time, consider these advantages and disadvantages.

Advantages

One of the largest advantages of Amazon FBA is its accessibility. That means that anyone can access Amazon and select your products without fear of running into scams or internet viruses. Along with its highly marketable platform, Amazon also works with you as a seller to create products that are better for you and your customers. These, among many other reasons, are why many people opt for a business with Amazon FBA.

When considering the advantages of any venture, always consider how well you will profit from the collaboration. Below are more examples of Amazon's excellent service and the advantages that come with becoming an Amazon FBA seller.

Logistics and Shipping

Even if you have never owned a store before, you have likely experienced the grueling sluggishness and painstaking process that is mail delivery. Little inconveniences like the wrong stamps or the incorrect weight of a package can prevent you from making deliveries on time, and busy times, such as those around the holidays, can slow your business to a stop while you try to keep up with the demand.

When sending packages for your own business, you have to think about how quickly your shipping will reach the customer and what rating you will receive if a package is late. Often, when products get lost in the mail or delivery is delayed, you are the one that receives the brunt of a customer's wrath. The logistics with shipping packages can become exceptionally difficult to maintain, and if you are not experienced with shipping packages, some items may not be sent at all.

When you are part of the Amazon FBA family, you no longer have to worry about shipping or the logistics that come from untimely package delivery. Amazon has shipped billions of products, so they know the procedure. Also, if a product is lost in the mail, Amazon will take care of the customer for you, giving you an extra payment for the merchandise lost.

Discounted Shipping Rates

Not only does Amazon handle the shipping of new products, but it also provides both customer and seller with major discounts. The major mail delivery companies that work with Amazon offer major discounts because of the many packages they deliver. This means that both customers and sellers profit from discounts.

Packages sent to Amazon in accord with Amazon FBA receive these discounts. Also, the two-day shipping that Amazon gives all Prime customers is a huge draw for customers. Those who come for the products may stay for the shipping. Its service is among the only of its kind. Shoppers with Amazon Prime subscriptions are more likely to shop, making your product line more accessible than ever.

Management of Returns

Returns are one of the most obnoxious parts of owning a business. Businessmen and women often have to shoulder the responsibility of paying for return shipping, refunds, and the cost it takes to send a new product if you are lucky.

You may be surprised to know that returns are more common than you would expect. Clothing is often returned because the online fitting is difficult. With Amazon's Prime Wardrobe, they handle returns often, as customers can send back clothing that does not fit or work for them. People also commonly return items that are broken or otherwise impaired. If a large chunk of your inventory has the same defect, the number of customers that return merchandise can explode.

Luckily, Amazon takes care of the dirty work for you when you sign up for Amazon FBA. The return shipping Amazon provides makes the task quick and easy, and you will see the changes to your store when the items are returned. Again, products are returned directly to Amazon, so you do not need to worry about additional shipping.

There is, however, a price to pay with return shipping. Amazon generally charges a fee every time a product is returned. The return fee is equal to the fulfillment fee, which you can calculate from Tables 3.1 and 3.2. Though that might seem like a pain, consider the advantages. Customer loyalty grows when they are offered free products or services, and free return shipping drives many shoppers to purchase merchandise on Amazon. When it comes down to the financials, letting Amazon take care of your returns really adds up in the bank. You will likely see a profit increase due to the number of products you are able to send in.

Customer Service Management

Dealing with customers is one of the leading causes of quitting jobs. Customers can be difficult to rein in when they have complaints, and it can become extremely discouraging to deal with people who do not like your product. Coupled with multiple returns, owning a business may not seem like the dream you believed it to be after all.

Amazon is one of the best customer service providers in the world. They have to be to get customers returning again and again. When you do not have to spend hours on the phone explaining why an order is not satisfactory, why not leave it to the professionals? With Amazon FBA, customers with complaints take their grievances directly to Amazon instead of bothering you.

Unlimited Storage Space

When developing an empire, storage space is one of the top necessities to keep your business running smoothly. Consider becoming a DVD or Blu-ray distributor, and your products are extremely popular due to the popularity of a recently released movie. To keep up with demand, you would need to either buy or rent a storage facility to take care of all your inventory. The costs for maintaining this storage facility may start to wipe you out, and understandably so. The more inventory you acquire, the greater the chance you have to make a profit, but it comes at a storage price.

Amazon has over 175 warehouses with over 150 million square feet to store your products (Amazon, n.d.). The only requirements to fulfill when storing products in the Amazon warehouses are listed in Table 3.3. Though there are fees associated with keeping products stored there, the price is far below what it would cost to rent a warehouse of your own.

Unlimited storage space is available for Amazon FBA sellers that are top in their class. Effectively, this means that if you are a high-profile seller with a high-performance score, you can provide Amazon with as many products as you want. This cost-efficient approach makes it easier for top sellers to maintain high statuses.

Quick Delivery

As with all Prime-eligible products, shipping is free and sends within two days. The faster products make it to your customers, the more likely they are to buy from your store again. Customers come to expect fast shipping, so shipping with Amazon ensures that you will be on top of the game.

Quick delivery has advantages for sellers in other ways as well. For instance, since products sent to Amazon with the Amazon FBA program receive discounted shipping costs, sellers can quickly stock inventory if the supply is low. If you are new to the business and do not know how much inventory to send to Amazon, the quick delivery to Amazon can get you out of a pinch.

Amazon's Multi-Channel Fulfillment (MCF)

Though commonly confused with Amazon FBA, Amazon's Multi-Channel Fulfillment uses Amazon to store products but send via third-party sites. For example, many FBA sellers have a website outside of Amazon; in fact, 80% of sellers do. This means that they are getting business from another site. Using the same principles as Amazon FBA, sellers that utilize MCF send all their products to Amazon who stores and distributes products, but all is done through personal business channels.

MCF is entirely dependent on outside sources. MCF users often use other selling sites to promote and sell merchandise; eBay is a common platform for MCF use. Sellers build loyalty with customers by offering the same shipping and service requirements that Amazon has, but merchants are not responsible for what happens to the product after it arrives at the Amazon facility.

Disadvantages

Though Amazon FBA has multiple benefits and advantages, it would not be a true company if it did not have its own rules. The disadvantages associated with Amazon FBA are often included with the advantages. Though there are wonderful perks, many come at a price. The only way to determine if selling with Amazon FBA is the right fit for you is to weigh the advantages and disadvantages.

Fees and Costs

If products stay in Amazon warehouses instead of selling, they will ultimately cost you a bundle in sky-high costs.

Have you ever wondered how some people can afford the prices at which they sell their products? Some merchandise on Amazon sells for only $2.00, way below what most would believe is a success. In this case, most people would be right. People cannot earn a profit on Amazon by selling products at extraordinarily low prices. While it may seem as though selling thousands of T-shirts at $2.50 each will pay off in the long run, many fail to realize not only the basic fees but also those that are buried under a long page of script.

Amazon has provided businesspeople with a calculator that will determine all fees associated with their products. However, many of these fees are estimated, and you may not always receive a clear picture of the charges. When determining what products to sell and how many, always round up. Even if you will not have to pay the higher prices, this will give you the maximum rate at which to sell products.

Storage fees may also seem like a small price to pay for signing up with one of the greatest selling platforms in the world, but consider how these fees can build up over time. For instance, if you sell miniature lizards that weigh approximately 2 oz., you may believe that the deal you get from storing them on Amazon far outweighs the small costs of storage. However, if you believe that your porcelain lizards will be the hit of the decade and you send 1,000 figurines to Amazon, the price for storing your merchandise starts to stack up. Even with the smallest weight class, it will cost you $690 each month to store your lizards, which only includes the months of January to September. As the holidays roll around, you will be paying $2,400 each month just for the storage.

Many people blindly start selling with Amazon FBA without doing research. Amazon FBA could seem like a rip-off if you are not careful about your products and market research. To prevent throwing away your money, take care of your inventory and keep an eye on marketing successes.

More Frequent Returns

Maintaining a strict policy on your website may prevent people from buying from your store, but offering fast and free returns increases the likelihood of more frequent returns. Since Amazon is known for its impeccable customer service, people are more likely to flock to the easy returns.

What does this mean for you? First, you will suffer the loss of a product that has not been sold, and you may have to continue to pay for its storage fees over time. Since you are charged for every return, the price for easier customer shipping also means that you are not seeing the same returns. If you are marketing a product that has size variations or inadequacies, you may see return fees build up quickly.

Difficult Product Prep

Though Amazon takes the guesswork out of handling products once they are received into warehouses, it does have rather strict guidelines for sending the merchandise. Any product that is not correctly labeled or sent to the right facility may be sent back at the seller's expense.

Trouble Tracking Inventory

When you run your own business, you can keep track of all inventory in and out of the shop. Receipts and order slips remind you who purchased what. Returns are handled by yourself or employees who know information about the customer, such as a phone number, email address, or the last four digits of a credit card. Shops that are run internally are designed to keep customer information for subsequent payments and to be a more personalized shop. It is not uncommon for a small business to know many of his or her customers by name.

Amazon FBA tracking, however, makes these connections much more difficult because, like most online stores, it does all of the above trackings for you. Much of your time as an Amazon FBA merchant is spent worrying about the products in terms of creating, shipping, packing, and making improvements. Though you may receive information from Amazon regarding product reviews, much of the personality of your business is exchanged for convenience.

It is not required to know the names of your customers, but when it comes to tracking packages, additional information is helpful for keeping track of orders. Amazon offers tools to make tracking easier, but it is still difficult to keep a handle on which orders went where and which customer left what review. If only one item was damaged, you may have to wade through multiple reviews to offer refunds or ask for product improvement, which takes a lot of precious time.

Difficult Sales Taxes

Keeping track of taxes can seem overwhelming for the smallest of businesses, but calculating tax with Amazon can become an absolute nightmare without help. Since Amazon is based in different states and countries, taxes vary. Even more frustrating, Amazon frequently moves products to different warehouses, changing the taxes on the products sold. Passing the road signs to even more complicated ground, you have to consider sales and shipping taxes. These also vary per state, and they might feel difficult to track with the range of different purchases.

Sales tax does not belong to the seller. Instead, the money collected from the tax goes directly to the states in which it is requested. But how do you keep track of which states need so much money? Amazon collects taxes for each state, but they do not give a clear pathway to set up payments to these states.

Various tools are set up to help you pay the right taxes for every state or country in which you do business. Amazon has its part in sellers' FBA accounts that shows what the taxes are for the states in which you sold merchandise. Unfortunately, you will either have to be an accountant or have access to software that will help you sort out all tax information and lay it out in a readable form.

Commingling

Commingling with Amazon FBA allows you to bunch your products with other sellers'. When you see a product on Amazon, often there are buying options that allow you to select from which seller to buy. People from all over the globe can add to a single product, often providing a large selection of products. Commingling can offer you more contact with your product, but there are problems with this system that can lead to serious charges held against you and anyone else in the commingling product sphere.

Have you ever searched for a product on Amazon and received something that looked nothing like the photo and had none of the specifications that were advertised on its page? The product you receive is likely from another company trying to stiff you by riding the coattails of a more successful product. Shoppers are taken in by the previous reviews of high-quality materials, and suddenly a flood of negative reviews may shut your shop down.

When participating in Amazon FBA commingling, you must be willing to take the risk that your high-quality products may not be the same as others. Even though the people reviewed your product and gave it a high rating, just as many, if not more, may try to make a quick buck. Always do your research when commingling, and provide an addendum to your product to ensure your customers receive the best quality and prices possible.

How To Sell Your Product?

By using Amazon FBA, your time is freed up to focus on increasing the visibility of your product while Amazon takes care of the rest- the packaging, the shipping, tracking as well as customer service.

You need to focus on marketing, advertising and promoting your product so it stands out from the 2.3 million other products vying for customer attention.

So how do you do that? When it comes to marketing your product, you can use many viable platforms such as creating your own website, writing a blog as well as using Facebook to advertise. Let's look into it!

Start A Blog

Having a blog for your online store is one of the best marketing components that you can have.

Not only would regular blogging increase your SEO rankings, but it also helps you build your brand and allows your customers to reach out to you on a different platform and get to know you or your brand on a more personal level.

Your blog can influence SEO as well as increase your customer connection. There are plenty of ready-to-go and easy-to-build blogs from WordPress to Blogspot, Tumblr to Medium that you can use.

The blogging sphere has come a long way with plenty of unique and easy to customize features. You can use this to write, edit as well as publish blog posts right from your admin panel.

Blog function seems to be useful for most merchants, especially those that have never had a blog before but if you have used a blog before or if you already have one, using WordPress or Blogger platforms offers the best blogging capabilities.

Effective Methods to Increase your Store's Visibility

There are many methods to use in online retail but in this chapter, we will look at the most effective methods that you can try in 2019.

I. Focus your time in Marketing

Many of the aspects in online retail are automated which frees up your time in focusing solely on branding and marketing your products as well as optimizing your site.

Marketing is a money maker so from the logo, website look and feel to the tone of voice- you want all these things to sync in well so that you can convert your traffic to sales.

Learn to master the use of ads, optimize your website with specific keywords. These elements drive more traffic to your store and convert at least 2% of customers on a daily basis.

Your objective is to get more traffic to your site so that it can generate a good percentage of sales. SEO can help drive long-term sales simply by having you rank high on search engine results. You can do this by:

1. Creating blog content
2. Optimizing your product pages
3. Update your pages and keep it fresh
4. Use Social media to optimize being found online

II. Create Fantastic Offers

Sales, bundles, and offers are something EVERYONE loves! It not only makes you noticeable but also increases traffic to your site!

If no products on your site are for sale, customers visiting your site will lack the motivation to purchase your products.

However, the right product with the right deal will more likely make them purchase on your site. Tie offers with celebrations or holidays or even create bundle packs.

When customers love a product from your site, they will most likely want to purchase more of it. The hardest part is to get them to purchase--after that, it is pretty uphill all the way!

III. Avoid Underpricing Your Products

In online retail, the cost of products is usually close to wholesale price and it allows you to sell your products at market value and get a nice profit. Businesses, whether online retail or dropshipping or otherwise is to make profits. If the cost of your product is $5 then you should be selling it for $20 so you can get profits.

If your prices are fair and within market value, you should be able to gain a sizable profit from each order made on your website.

Do not undercut your prices even when other retailers are doing so unless you are giving an offer or discount or a sale. Create strategies that will allow you to make more money overall.

IV. Choose ePacket

ePacket shipping is currently the fastest and most affordable online retail method. It ensures quick delivery without high costs. An ePacket shipping on average would cost you under $5 for most products so this will allow you to make a profit when you sell your product at market value.

ePacket deliveries reach customers within 7 to 10 days from the date of purchase and are by far one of the best delivery methods for online retailers to use.

V. Go the extra mile with customer service

As anyone going to a restaurant if they would go back to a restaurant if the food was mediocre but with exceptional service, chances are that the answer would be yes. People remember more of how you made them feel and the same applies to e-commerce as well.

Offering great customer service is one of the best ways to stand out especially if you are selling the same products are every merchant out there.

Your customer service can be in the form of thank you cards included in the shipping packages or it could also be points that they have accumulated from multiple purchases which entitle them to a free gift!

It can also be simple things like a speedy response to their issues or complaints. Whatever you do, make your customers feel valued and appreciated - it is because of them that you are a success.

VI. Stay active on your channels

You need to put in effort on a consistent and daily basis.

While you do not need to spend eight hours a day working on marketing and promoting your site, you still need to commit a number of hours on a daily basis to ensure that your store is updated, relevant and active.

As your business grows, so will the number of hours you need to commit to processing orders, speak with your suppliers, ensure shipping is in route and orders arrive promptly to your customers.

You will also need to ensure that your marketing efforts are in line with your products and social media is one of the best ways to stay current and relevant, ensuring that you appear at least once a day in the minds of your customers.

VIII. Monitor your competition

As always, you need to keep your friends close and your enemies closer. Monitor your competition's social media and their websites regularly.

Like their page and you'll also receive updates on their products and the promotions they have.

By paying attention to what they do, you'll also have a better idea of how to sell your products on your store. Do not rip-off content but use it as inspiration to understand what makes or breaks attention.

This not only helps bring in the audience to your site but it also helps you make you do better in marketing your products.

Optimizing your website for e-commerce

A site optimized for e-commerce is extremely crucial even if you use the Amazon FBA model. There are plenty of platforms that you can use which are all very simple and features drag & drop capabilities such as SquareSpace and Wix.

Of course, you can also get a web design and development company to help you create an e-commerce website, should you have a sizable budget for this. However, many newbie retailers prefer using play-and-play e-commerce, especially in the beginning.

You can then explore additional website customization once you have a better idea of where your business is heading, have better funds and add in new approaches to your site.

Do you need an e-commerce website if you sell on Amazon FBA?

The answer is YES if you want more out of your business and the answer is NO if you are just happy with the way things are and have no intention of expanding. It depends on what your business goals are.

However, having an e-commerce website that operates outside of Amazon it one of the ways to increase the visibility of your product and enable it to sell more.

Here are some reasons why having an e-commerce site is crucial:

- You get to explore more ways of selling your product other than what Amazon offers and implement more varied strategies

- You can build brand equity

- You can build a solid customer base and an email list

- You can advertise and increase your reach

- You can generate B2B sales

- You have better product flexibility on your own site

Why is it important to optimize your site?

Someone types out an item on Google search that is sold in your store.

Unless your product's page has been optimized properly, this person may not be able to find your products or your store easily.

Unless you want to miss out on potential customers, you must make optimizing your site a priority.

Understanding Product Keyword Research and its Importance

Each product page that you created on your site needs to be supported by research in the eyes of the buyers who search for your product.

This is the reason why keyword research is important when it comes to SEO. Before you optimize your page, you must know the keywords that are used to search for your type of product and what attracts the most traffic.

As a site owner for an Amazon business, you must understand the unique and best keywords and phrases used for your products by factoring these elements:

- relevance, search volume, and ranking difficulty.

You can use tools such as Google Search Console to help you identify the top queries on the net, Unamo SEO for analyzing the competition, Keywordtool.io to gain insight on consumer behavior as well as Google Keyword Planner for finding product page keywords that you can target.

Ensure Your Product Names Are Relevant and Descriptive

When naming your product, you have to ensure that they are to-the-point and also include descriptions that your customers will want to know about your product. The easiest way to do this is to do a Google search of the product you are selling and see what kinds of description and product names are used on the most visible pages.

- Add Value to Your Products with High-Quality Descriptions

Product descriptions are extremely valuable with SEO but only when it is value-added. Your product descriptions that your customers would want to know about the product such as Key Features and Specifications, major features and value. You can also include model numbers, keyword variation, and brand name.

Ultimately, you also want to keep these descriptions brief yet informative but not extremely wordy. Bullet points and lists are extremely favored. Also, never copy content from the manufacturer- you want to make yours unique to your dropshipping site.

- Improve Rankings with Your Page Title

Another way to optimize your site is to include the right page titles that correspond to your product as well as boost click-through rates. Your page title has to be unique and includes relevant keywords. Start by placing the main keyword at the front of the title but do not repeat it. Your brand name should also be included in the title for maximum effect.

- Have Unique Meta Descriptions for All Items

Keywords included in meta descriptions do not affect rankings but you need to add them anyways as it can bring in more clicks. On top of that, including keywords and formatting them with numbers and symbols can also boost click-through rates immensely.

Explain what is present on the page and give information to users on what they are clicking on. Again, do make it unique but do not make it lengthy. Push forth the key selling points of the product to boost click-through rates and use numbers, prices and other formatting options to make your product stand out. Shopify, the favored dropshipping site provides a simple and intuitive editor to make changes to metadata. It also automatically generates robots.txt and sitemap.xml files to prevent duplicate content problems.

- Pay Attention to Product URLs

URLs are sometimes the least looked into optimization element. Clean and keyword-friendly URLs make huge impacts on search rankings. If you have old URLs, make sure they are redirected to the new URLs on your site. Your URLs must be user-friendly and appear directly beneath the title in search engine results.

Again, these URLs must be short and written all in lowercase, they must include keywords as well as subfolders. Do not include any dynamic parameters and clean up elements that are unnecessary in the URL structure such as ID categories.

- Add Product Reviews

Product reviews are an ultimate must for a site. It builds trust and enables user engagement as well. When enabling product reviews for your site, make sure that the text is crawlable.

You also need variety on your reviews--not all of them are going to be five-star and that's okay. The variety of feedback gives legitimacy for your products. You can get user reviews through email follow-ups, incentivizing on user interaction at the same time offering discounts and raffles to those that submit feedback.

- Improve Your Chances with Videos and Images

When creating your site, use quality product videos and images. How-to videos and 360 images of your product increase buy-in and it also compliments your keywords, headings, and product descriptions. It also boosts your sales and traffic.

Quality images and videos also give credibility to your site. When including photos and videos, optimize them by using keywords in the file name and alt tags. Optimization can also be done through video and image sitemaps that ensure your product's pages are crawled quickly and effectively.

- Reduce the Loading Time of Product Pages

At this day and age, flashy graphics and slow loading pages are a big NO. User's attention span is 3 seconds and when they visit your site, they want to see the products that they are interested in without waiting for a long video to be over or pop-ups clouding their vision. Test your optimized site using the Pingdom's Performance monitoring tool to see how fast your page loads.

How to Sell Like Crazy

1. Introduction to Amazon Ads

Amazon has paid marketing specifically created for sellers that want to showcase their products to potential customers. Whenever someone types a search term in the Amazon search bar, organic and inorganic listings will show up.

Usually, sponsored listings are placed on the top of the result page. So, there's a huge scope to create ads for your products. If you want to gain visibility of your new or old products, then creating ads is the best practice.

Although this service offered by Amazon is paid, and you will be charged whenever someone clicks and buys your product. But this charge is worth paying. Because the profit you will make is much higher than the charge of paid marketing on Amazon.

No matter what your niche is, if you want your customers to buy your product as soon as you source the product on the shopping window then utilizing Amazon ads is the best step. But you have to start with some rules and strategies. Don't put a random product on sponsored ads. If you have a slight idea that a product is getting some sales, then apply ads to it. But never waste your money on ads for an extremely new product.

Applying PPC ads on Amazon products is also beneficial in improving organic rankings. Because through sponsored ads, sale history gets improved and as a result product ranks better in Amazon SERPs.

You might be wondering how much you have to spend in order to rank better on Amazon. Well, let me tell you it is extremely affordable. On average you have to spend $0.35 per click.

Amazon ads are divided into two categories: Self-serve ads and premium ads.

The self-serve ads are displayed like Google search ads. On the other hand, premium ads are shown like display ads. Display ads are placed on the sidebar as visual banners.

Pay per click is PPC. Every time someone clicks on your listing, you get charged. There is an automatic campaign and a manual campaign. An automatic campaign means that Amazon is choosing random keywords from your product listing and placing it in front of customers who are typing in those keywords. Amazon is choosing random keywords from your listing and advertising on their website. For example, if someone is shopping for a beach ball but they are shopping for a blue beach ball and you have an automatic campaign going, it will show up because it has this keyword in it.

2. Unconventional Channels To Boost Your Sales

You can boost the sales on Amazon by utilizing various channels. There can be multiple channels to improve the sales but I have narrowed down some of the most useful channels for you.

1. Social Media – The most useful channel to boost sales is through social media. You can leverage the sales through videos on YouTube, or posts on Facebook, or tweeting the product links on Twitter. Or better, post the product images on Instagram. How can this be helpful to boost sales? As you may know, most of the internet visitors are regular on these social media platforms. And you can utilize these channels to reach your target customers. Create pages for your online store and regularly post the product listing URLs. There are many Facebook groups where you can share the products.

2. Affiliate – Do you want to utilize the profit for another paid promotion? Then try to sell the products through affiliates. These affiliates can be a company or individual that sells the product in exchange for a commission. Don't just settle for an affiliate for the sake of sales. Evaluate any affiliate before start doing business with them.

3. Influencers – In the era of online influence, people often consider the recommendation of a person who has a good standing on a social media platform. You should find an influencer that has huge followers and is specialized in your industry.

4. Forums – There are relevant forums on the internet which can be joined to spread the word about your product. You can either join general forums or forums that are specifically for your niche.

3. SEO Strategies

What Is SEO And Why Is Important

It is more important than ever that you pay close attention to search engine optimization. Why? Because there are over 3.5 billion searches per day on Google alone! And billions more on other search engines like YouTube, Amazon & Bing. Each and every one of those people are looking to learn about something or buy something. And if you're not showing up you are losing out on a huge opportunity. I am going to tell you precisely what SEO is and why you need it by sneaking you behind the scenes of some sites. I'll also be sharing how long it takes to see results and I'll tell you how to do it without spending any money.

Sound good? Great! Because search engine optimization is all about making sure that your website shows up when people are searching. This is absolutely critical for businesses and website owners in the digital age. Why? Because if you solution to the problem that is been searched for, then the chance to be pushed in front of thousands of people. example: If you owned a hardware store and your website was the #1 result in Google for "buy power tools", you would generate thousands of dollars per day in sales revenue.

That is because SEO is the most effective method to boost sales or website and its revenue. With targeted SEO you can capture thousands of searchers to your website or product every day. I want to tell you a secret. All you need to start seeing positive growth in search engines is a little SEO knowledge and know-how.

Honestly, if you're not using SEO as part of your strategy to grow your business or website, you're missing out on thousands of people and thousands of dollars every single month! And the daft thing is that SEO doesn't have to cost a lot of money. SEO can be done without a lot of money and there are plenty of free tools to search for keywords and optimize a website or product.

Now don't get me wrong, if you make small investments in tools like Ahrefs or SEMRush you would be able to accelerate your results. But my point is this if you are just starting out, SEO doesn't have to be expensive and, in most niches, you can gain traction by learning the basics of SEO and then applying it to your site. And you might be wondering how long does it take see results if you do that? Well, honestly there isn't really a right or wrong answer to this question. You will typically start seeing results from SEO within the first 4 weeks.

And by results, I mean positive movement in search rankings and visibility in Amazon SERPs. If you don't see any positive movement in those first 4 weeks then something might be wrong and it would be worth using the site audit tools from Ahrefs or SEMRush to help find the problem.

So now you know exactly what SEO is, why you need SEO and what SEO can do for you. It is the most effective way of finding new business, customers and traffic. Especially if you're a small business or just starting out! Don't forget that you can learn and apply the basic principles of SEO without spending anything.

You just need to understand one thing. You have to optimize the product listing to get more sales. This optimization will

Now that you know what is SEO, you must know why is SEO important. Amazon has its algorithm to rank the products. This algorithm is called A9. When your product listing is optimized according to the algorithm, you will get more visitors. And these visitors will tend to buy the products. These purchases will result in more profit.

How to Use The Perfect Strategy to Improve Your Ranking on Amazon

Just as the users search their query on Google when they need to search something, they also search the product they want to buy on Amazon. And as there are SERPs (search engine result pages) on Google, there are SERPs on Amazon as well. And most of the visitors or buyers don't bother visiting the second or third page of the SERP.

How can you optimize the listing so that the listings are placed on the first page of Amazon? Through optimizing. Amazon's SEO is somewhat different from that of Google. You don't need a website to optimize Amazon listing, but many other factors are similar. For example, keywords and content need to be optimized on both platforms.

Amazon works on the algorithm named A9. Almost hundreds of millions of searches are done on Amazon every month. And Amazon has to decide which is the most appropriate result for that query. Thus, you have to become really upfront to optimize the product listing page.

Amazon ranks the product on the basis of this factor:

How much purchase likelihood the product has?

If your product has no relevant content when it comes to purchasing likelihood, then that product will not be ranked. Optimizing Amazon product works organically. You can't use any black-hat method to rank on Amazon. The listing should have relevant information that a user is looking for.

Taking all of these things into account, Amazon ranks the product on 1 which is most likely to sell and on rank 2 which is less likely to sell and so on. Now you must know how Amazon filters out an appropriate listing for a search query.

So, the first factor is the keyword and another factor is performance. If your product listing has a keyword that is relevant to the query, then the listing will be shown on SERPs. The performance of the listing is calculated on the ranking factor. This is based on many things like images, reviews, ads, price, traffic, product copy, inventory, Prime/FBA, and more.

To find out whether your product ranks for the keyword or not, run a search for the keyword related to your product. If your product doesn't appear for that keyword, it's the time to optimize the listing.

You can take Amazon PPC into account to check the ranking of a product. You can check CTR (click-through rate) and CR (conversion rate) to measure how your listing performs for a search query.

How can you optimize the listing?

1. Optimize the content – The content on your product page is the magnet to attract the customers to buy that product. Content can be anything like title, description, image, and bullet points. You should create a persuasive title, an in-depth description,

brand content, additional information, and images that look professional. The brand story can highlight what is your business and everything about your other products. It even creates a sense of brand awareness among customers. And in addition to that, you can even mention other products that are available to the customers.

2. Images – High-quality images are the key to selling quickly on Amazon. Images play a huge role in improving the CR and CTR of a listing. An image is the first thing that your customers will see on the product page. You can upload images in JPEG or PNG formats but make sure these images are of high quality. The customer must be able to see every part of the product by zooming in.

3. Mention The Size – There can be some products where it is essential to mention the size. You can use the images and product descriptions both to mention the size of the product. It adds credibility to your brand and products.

4. Keywords – You can search keywords through various methods. The first method is to use Amazon autocomplete. Search a keyword on the search tab and check what kind of queries are available for your product. Another method is to use competitor

listings. Type in the search query related to your product and check the top most results. Find out which main keywords they are using to rank better in the Amazon SERPs. Reviews are also the best method to find which are the words used by the customers. When you are done finding the keywords, it's the time to add these to your listings. You can add the keywords in the title, descriptions, bullet points, brand story, keywords, backend keywords, and product information field.

5. Price – Whenever you consider pricing the products, make sure you check what your competitors are charging for that product. You should beat your competitors when it comes to pricing. Never charge too much for a product as it is not beneficial.

6. Maintenance – Kudos to you if you have reached until this step of optimization of your listing. Always remember listing optimization is not a one-step process. You have to maintain this optimization to rank better on the marketplace. Always reply to the reviews of the customers and if possible, apply the paid promotion to the listings whenever possible. Other than that, you must always pay close attention to the shipping and inventory methods of the products.

4. Your Customers Are Your Best Friends

How to Create a Perfect Customer Care

Do you want to build a business that no one can beat? Then start building a rapport with your customers. Your customer is the most loyal entity associated with your business. If you are able to please and maintain a long-term relationship with your customer, then you can be the most successful business in your industry.

There some major tactics involved to become a business that everyone loves. I will be disclosing those tactics to you right away.

1. Build The Business On The Foundation Of Customer Service – If you start a business to serve your customers, then you will stay committed to this mission forever. Don't think about profit all the time. After you have calculated all the profits, think about how you can improve the lives of your customers. Then stick to this plan. Whenever you deal with the customers, be helpful to them while solving their problems.

2. The Customer-Centric Business – The culture of your business should be built around listening to customers. Everyone in the customer care department should be willing to listen to the

customers. By listening I mean your customer care staff should pay close attention to what the customer is saying while they have any problem. If you can listen to their problems patiently, I bet there won't be any unhappy customers.

3. Provide Essential Information on Product Listing - Your customer is not always willing to dwell on customer care. They want to know everything before or after purchasing the product. If you can provide essential information even before they have a query, then it will be encouraging for the customers. The product listing should be easily navigated through. And all the relevant information should be readily available on the product or brand page itself.

4. Human Interaction - The customer care team of your company should be willing to provide real-time information about whatever a customer needs to know. The interaction should be as easy if a customer is talking in-person with the customer care executive. There should not be any miscommunication whatsoever. The assistance over the phone is much better than the automated emails. It ensures how much you value your customers.

5. Email Customer Service - The turnaround time to reach the customers should easily available on your brand page. If the customers are sending you emails and you are only sending automated replies, then this can be a huge turn-off. Instead, have a dedicated team to assist the customers through emails. Remember? Human interaction is really important to stay connected with customers.

How to Squeeze Your Customers Via Email for Other Sales

Your customers are buying some of your products and you are willing to sell other products too. Every seller has this wish and that's where email marketing helps. Suppose you get a new sale and you are just happy with the profit you just earned.

Don't settle for less. Collect the emails through Amazon central and keep your customers informed and engaged at every step. You can send them thank you emails when they purchase something. Be there with them at each step. Or you can send them personalized coupons to buy a product from your range.

Another option is to ask for a review when they have purchased a product. This continuous process is mandatory to remind a customer that there are actual sellers behind Amazon. Do whatever it takes, but keep them engaged in your product range.

How To Create And Optimize The Perfect Product Page

Branding Your Products on Amazon

Since you have placed the order for your products, it's now time to prepare them for sale. You probably are thinking of things related to packing, labeling, and sending your products over to Amazon's fulfillment centers. But product preparation involves a lot more than that, so you also need to consider branding. This is a fundamental aspect, as you will need to make sure that nothing can stop you to sell these products on Amazon so you have the rights to sell them. When you are a third-party reseller, selling products on this platform can get more complicated than you anticipated.

This is why you will need to consider the following scenarios:

Lately, there have been quite a few cases of unauthorized sellers that caught the attention of Amazon. By unauthorized sellers, I mean merchants who continue to sell on this platform although they don't have the rights to do so. It may happen that you don't have full control over your inventory, meaning your products can fall into the wrong hands, so there might be some merchants selling your products without your approval. Obviously, you are not seeing a dime of these sales, so this is where things can get problematic. Unfortunately, not everyone selling on this platform complies with Amazon policies.

It's really hard to imagine something worse for a brand than the situation when there is price transparency, but the authorized sellers don't have command over the price. You might be selling your product at a determined price, and suddenly comes another merchant who sells your own product at a lower price, even though you didn't allow him to do so. Customers are very influenced by the price, so if the product is identical, he will buy cheaper, and not from you.

Fortunately for you, there is a way to avoid this nightmare. You can find a way to protect your brand on Amazon and avoid your products being sold without your consent. This is why you should register a trademark. However, in some cases this may not be enough, so you will need to get some legal counseling to come up with a "bulletproof" trademark. There are still scenarios where the unauthorized sellers can get away with selling your products, but this is where your legal counseling should make the difference. A common practice for the unauthorized sellers is to invoke the "first sale doctrine," which apparently is a legal concept that can allow anyone in a country to buy a product and resell it to whoever (and whenever) they want. This doesn't sound fair, does it?

There are so many different ways to define and implement a trademark capable of protecting you from any unauthorized sellers, especially when they invoke the first sale doctrine. Therefore, to tighten your trademark, you will need to follow the guidelines mentioned below:

1. Tighten your grip over the distribution process so you don't have to send cease-and-desist letters to any unauthorized resellers.
2. Demonstrate that the continued sale of your products without your approval is a legal issue.

It's hard to think of any brand that has absolute control over their distribution process, so their products might fall into the hands of these kinds of merchants. However, by following the tips mentioned above you can aim to minimize this issue, so you will benefit from the sales of your products.

Advertising on Amazon

We have to admit that using just pure SEO techniques will not help you too much nowadays as most likely every merchant on this platform (at least the serious ones) is working hard to optimize the content. But where SEO has its limits, advertising can come along and help you to boost your product visibility and rankings. Using paid advertising will get you the views you need, but you need to make these views worth it to seriously increase your conversion rate. Optimized content will help, but the most decisive aspect that turns a view into a sale is the feedback.

Advertising has the job of promoting your product, but it's not forcing users to buy the product. But to understand the duality of advertising, you might want to check the lines below:

- The PPC (Pay-per-Click) element is the first phase of the sale since it makes merchants bid on keywords to secure a very good spot on the page. PPC Advertising makes a lot of money for Amazon, so you can understand why this company is allowing third-party resellers to trade on this platform. It's absolutely normal for Amazon to make a large portion of its money from this PPC Advertising process.
- The second phase is when the displayed product gets sold, so the view turns into a sale (a process called conversion). Guess what! Amazon charges a fee for many sales on this platform, and again the company wins a lot of money.

In fact, Amazon manages to score a triple win, if you really think about it, as it:

- Helps the user to find the best match for the product that he or she is seeking, so the platform gets more users, and more people willing to spend their money.
- Boosts the rankings of the seller based on the searched items (PPC Advertising, plenty of money here).

- Takes a fee for sales (if they are done from Individual Accounts).

Increased competition has convinced many sellers to use paid advertising, otherwise, they couldn't be one step in front of the rest. In the past, organic SEO was simply enough to have a better ranking and eventually more sales. But different needs require different solutions, so there has to be a way to differentiate the merchants on this platform as most of them are already optimizing heavily their content. Some of them have become extremely skilled at running paid advertising campaigns just by following the principles below:

- Finding the best keywords to bid on
- Bidding wisely
- Using higher and higher budgets for advertising
- Using experts for this kind of service

An advertising campaign will not guarantee you incredibly high sales, as we are not talking about an exact science. There are plenty of factors that can influence your sales, and advertising plays a key role in this whole process. This is why you will need to find ways to maximize the efficiency of each advertising campaign. There are three types of advertising you can use on this platform, as you can see below:

- Sponsored Product Ads are the most common way of advertising on this platform. You can benefit from this option if you are using a Vendor Central or a Seller Central account. You bid on the right keywords and when the user is typing something in the search query, if your product keywords are relevant to the search query, your product will be displayed in a very convenient position. You are paying for every click users are making, and when your clicks run out, the product will be removed from the Sponsored Product Ads part. Therefore, if you are paying for customers to get on your product page (this is why it's called Sponsored Product Ads), why not make those clicks count. The ideal situation is to convert most of these clicks into sales, but this is also up to your content, price and, most of all, reviews.

- Sponsored Brands Ads is quickly becoming a more popular option for some brand-registered merchants who sell on Amazon. The product placement opportunities are a bit different, but the link will get users to the Brand page (not the product page). This type of keyword bidding will be more focused on the brand. Obviously, this kind of advertising is to increase the overall sales of the brand, not just for a specific product.

- Sponsored Display Ads can show up on your competitor's page and are designed to steer traffic away from your competitor's page to yours. It may not be a very common form of advertising, but it's still used by some sellers on this platform.

It can become very expensive if several merchants bid on exactly the same bids. Although you might be tempted to secure the position no matter the cost, keep in mind that your campaigns will have to be efficient, so perhaps it's better to back off when you are caught in a bidding war with your competitors. You have to think if the current value of the bid is worth it before going ahead with the bidding process.

I will focus more on the Sponsored Product Ads, as this form of advertising is more universal, and it's used by most of the sellers present on the Amazon platform. If you are still hesitant about paying for advertising to increase your sales, perhaps the following lines will change your mind, as some of the main advantages of this method can be seen below:

1) It can be the best way to introduce a new product in the marketplace. Sponsored Product Ads can steer traffic to your product page and seriously increase the visibility of your products. It's the help you need to boost your sales, see your profits growing and reviews adding up.

2) It's decisive when it comes to boosting your rankings and your sales.

Today, you can't hope to be present on the first page of the results, if you are just using Organic SEO unless you are already a veteran of this niche market. This is why you need all the help you can get, so this form of advertising can be exactly what you need. When your product is becoming more visible, it generates more sales, and thus it will get higher rankings. At one point, you will not depend so much on advertising to get sales, as your product can run on "organic sales" as well.

3) It's perhaps the best tool to lure new customers.

When your product is placed on the top side of the first page, users will click on it because your product matches their intention, it probably has a very good price, and it looks good. Chances are that the view can turn into a sale, so you really can't hope for more.

4) Sponsored Product Ads are significantly contributing to your sales.

You probably know the search habits of most users on the Amazon platform. Would you search for your favorite product on the 10th or 20th page of the results pages? Sponsored Product Ads will guarantee you a spot on these first pages, right on top of the pages, so the potential customers will see first your link. Clicks will lead to more views, and these views will lead to more sales. You can say that this is like a domino effect, as more sales will lead to more reviews and more reviews will generate even more sales.

As the Prime community grows as we speak, merchants will go the extra mile to make their products more visible. Sponsored Product Ads is the best and simplest method at their disposal, and the abuse of advertising made some specialists say that Amazon has become an advertocracy, as merchants have to pay now in order to exist or survive in this marketplace.

If you are not using Sponsored Product Ads, you might need to think again, as you are:

- Providing a great advantage for your competitors

- Leaving the best spots for product placement to them

- You are saving money while your competitors are getting more sales (are making a lot more money than you), reviews, and better rankings

Probably the lines above will make you rush to bid on keywords to get your products placed on the best spots. However, you may need to avoid the following scenarios:

- Spending too much money on bids to secure the sweet spot on the first page (your campaign will not be that effective, as you pay too much to make a sale)

- Your competitor might use the same data as you are, and you can find yourself in a bidding war against your competitor for the exact keywords. Remember, you are using the same source (the Amazon platform)

- Speaking of bidding wars, guess who gets to win the most when you have to place very high bids to secure your spot on the first page? All the increased advertising costs will only make Amazon tons of money.

But don't let the facts above discourage you, as nothing is perfect, but when you draw the line, you will easily see that this option has a lot more benefits than downsides. If you are now convinced to run a Sponsored Product Ads Campaign, you will need to consider the following aspects:

Campaign Name

You will need to select a proper campaign name that has to be very descriptive, but also very easy to remember.

Target ACoS

You are probably wondering what ACoS stands for. It literally means the Average Costs of Sales, an indicator developed by Amazon to show the cost-effectiveness of your campaign. In plain words, it represents how much you spend on an advertising campaign to generate a sale (caused by this advertising campaign). The ideal situation is when this indicator is lower. Some specialists would consider a very good value 25%. The result is the ratio between the money you spent on a campaign and the revenue generated by the campaign.

Automatic Targeting Type

You can use technology to find the most popular keywords, so the algorithm will automatically find out the most relevant keywords to your (and your competitor's) product listings. Investing too much in this targeting type is definitely not recommended, so it's recommended to use only a small portion of your advertising budget on automatically targeted keywords. This targeting type is more like a lottery, as you don't have too much control over the results.

Manual Targeting Type

If you want more control over the keywords that you will search for, then you need to go for the manual targeting type. There are tools out there that can come up with millions of different keywords, but you only need to select the match type–if you prefer broad, phrase, or exact match. The match type will only increase the relevance of the search, therefore, the exact match is the most powerful targeting type.

Daily Budget

This represents the amount of money you are willing to spend per day on an advertising campaign. If you want to focus on auto-target campaigns, then you should only spend between $5 and $10 per day on such campaigns. However, if you plan to run a manual targeting campaign, then you will need to increase your daily budget to around $20 for the beginning and then run slight increases over time.

Ad Groups

This aspect is about setting different important facts, like the keywords you would like to bid on (or the ones you want to avoid), match type or default bids.

Most specialists would agree that you will need to place a lower amount of money on auto-target keywords, but still, you need to be the judge of that. To make things a bit easier, you can see below the advantages of auto-target campaigns:

- It's fast and easy
- Amazon provides you a huge list of keywords obtained through a very big data collection process
- Most likely you will get the keywords you were thinking of

However, to make a wise decision, you need to know the downsides of this method as well:

- Less control, but the process is easy enough
- Less relevant keywords, so this can affect you

- Perhaps the only reason why Amazon is still keeping this method is that it generates a huge number of possible keywords, and every word can lead to a click, so more money-making possibilities for Amazon

Now, let's find out why the manual-target search is much more recommended. Depending on the match type, the manual-target search can be divided into the following types:

- Broad match, which is a form that includes some specified keywords regardless of their order, allowing for other words to be between the keywords (before or after). This is the widest form of manual-target search, and it doesn't provide the best results. In this case, the search may not be that relevant, so it can drive away your potential customers (or possibly they might be curious enough to check your product).

- Phrase match is a sequence of words capable of pairing with the user search terms. It can deliver better results than the previous version, as the search is a lot more relevant. So, there are higher chances of increasing the conversion rate.

- Exact match really doesn't need further explanation, as the keywords you selected will match exactly the ones typed in by the user. You really can't hope for a higher relevance, so the conversion rate is extremely high in this case.

- Negative keywords are just the keywords you want to avoid, and not to bid on. They should be discovered in the Ad Group phase of the Sponsored Ads campaign.

Most specialists would recommend you to diversify, so as "not to put your eggs in one basket." This means that your daily budget will have to be split between auto-target generated keywords and manual-target search. It's easy to tell that the auto-target one doesn't deliver the best results, so you need to spend less money on it and more money on the manual target ones. Now it's up to you on which match type you invest the most, but I would probably go with exact and phrase match.

Pack It And Ship It

Success on Amazon FBA depends on a lot of factors. You've got your clients, suppliers, marketing, advertising, and one other essential aspect, your inventory. More specifically, the way you manage your inventory. Order fulfillment issues can spell disaster for your business. Order volumes are never consistent. Sometimes you get more sales coming in, and sometimes you get less. It can be tricky trying to gauge what the right amount of orders is all the time. This is why you need a good inventory management strategy to help you juggle the order fulfillment issues and help you maintain the right stock levels so you're never overstocked or understocked.

Managing Your Inventory

Meeting customer demand and keeping your customers happy is one of the many crucial success factors that will determine how well your Amazon FBA business thrives. In order to meet the demand, you need to have inventory on hand at all times full stop in doing so your customer satisfaction levels improve significantly, and along with it, your ratings as a seller. With customers expecting more and more out of businesses these days, having a well-managed inventory is now more crucial than it has ever been. Amazon themselves have introduced in long-term storage option for the inventory that happens to be slow-moving.

As a new seller, it is normal to have questions and concerns about managing your FBA inventory. Inventory management goes beyond just making sure that you have enough stock on hand all the time as soon as the orders come in. Management in this context includes forecasting your sales, the volume of orders, cash flow, and sellers need to also maneuver the process of staying on top of Amazon's search listings. You will also need to focus on promoting your sales. A common concern among sellers is how impossible Amazon makes it maintain healthy stock levels. Payment needs to be made twice a month to the platform which may slow down the ordering and paying process for inventory. That makes it even more crucial to figure out how to manage your inventory effectively so you could make it easier for yourself to keep track and stay on top.

Amazon is not the only E-Commerce platform where running out of stock means you are going to lose out on a specific sale at a specific time. This happens in almost every selling situation outside of Amazon. The biggest issue would be the loss of a sale because on Amazon. The implications of going out of stock could potentially be long-term and negative, to say the least. Your future sales could be affected because your ranking drops in the search listings. When customers are unhappy and frequently experience out of stock situations when they come to your store, they are going to eventually divert to your competition. This is a very serious issue if you are selling a fast-moving consumer product in your store. Besides your reputation taking a beating, these are the other potential problems you could run into when your inventory is poorly managed:

- Losing Sales Means Losing Income - You cannot sell when you have run out of items to sell. When you're not selling, you're not making money. The results are even more detrimental when you do not have stock on Amazon compared to if you run out of stock on your own e-commerce website. Why? Because on Amazon, there is no back-ordering option that you could provide to your customers the way you would be able to if you were running your own online store. On your website, you are in control. You can still take backorders, and your listing will not go down. You can also notice that an item is out of stock and let your customers know its expected arrival date. But on Amazon, you do not have such flexibility. That said, you can manipulate this to your advantage by making the ordering process a little bit longer for the items that are still in stock, especially when you already know when your stock will come. This just helps you maintain a flowing system of sales and order. When your stock is at zero, your listing is going to drop. Sales for the product you are selling will continue your competitors' page. Until you have restocked, and you're able to get your sales moving again, your listing is going to continue being affected when you're out of inventory.

- Low Product Rankings - Amazon's customers expect instant shipping or a maximum of 3 days for their product to arrive on their doorstep. If you extend your product ordering process by up to 7 days, for example, this may cause your customers to become unhappy enough with your service to go elsewhere. Going out of stock once or twice is ok, sometimes, it happens despite your best efforts. However, if you regularly go out of stock for long periods of time, this is going to be terrible for your reputation. This is going to affect your search results, Amazon's algorithm depends on a variety of factors when they calculate search engine listing results, and among the most important factors would be product availability. When what you're selling is out of stock, your listings are not going to show up each time a customer searches for your product on Amazon. If you happen to go out of stocks or often, your listings as a seller are going to eventually come tumbling down. If the products you are selling happens to be unique items with less competition, going out of stock might not affect your search results that much if it happens once in a while, full stop, it is only products with a vast number of competitors that will see their search rankings quickly drop lower and lower.

- No Reviews and Poor Reviews - Reputation is everything when you're on a major E-Commerce site like Amazon. Reviews are the number one reason why a customer today which was to buy from you over everyone else. You could do all your marketing right, but when the customer comes to your page and reads nothing but poor reviews under your product listing, they are going to immediately change their mind about buying from you. All the great marketing tactics in the world are not going to be enough to convince them to buy from you if the feedback that they see is primarily negative. Ratings and reviews are one of the Amazon sellers' many lifelines. When your reviews are amazing, your search results are amplified, and you emerge at the top of the search results rankings. When this happens, you are able to attract new buyers and convert that traffic into sales. Therefore, you simply cannot risk running out of stock so often because it is going to severely impact the way you are perceived by your customers.

Amazon's Inventory Management Tracking System

Amazon has provided sellers with inventory management tools that help you keep track of specific information that is important to your business. It is crucial to know the inventory features that Amazon provides when you become an Amazon seller. If Amazon thinks there is specific information that is important enough to be made available for sellers, then you should make it matter to you too. You do have the option of using third-party systems to help you manage your inventory, syncing the data to your Seller Central dashboard too. Even if you do choose to use a third-party source, it is still important to know the data and information given to you by Amazon. You can access your inventory data by going to the Manage

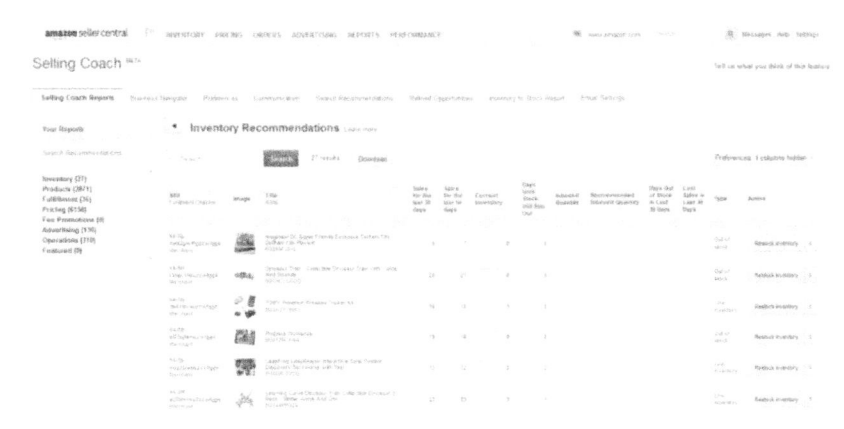

Inventory option:

Image Source: Repricer Express

Since manually tracking your Inventory on spreadsheets or documents is too time-consuming with the danger of making too many mistakes, Amazon's inventory management software is the answer to that conundrum. This is by far the best way to automate and manage all the tasks related to your inventory so that you are carrying just enough stock without being overstocked. FBA retailers see almost a 40% increase in management efficiency when they rely on this software to get it done. The best part is this Seller Central dashboard already has all the in-built tools that you need available for free.

Within your account dashboard alone, you'll be able to see the Amazon Selling Coach option that reports all the key data related to your inventory that you need to know. You'll be able to get an overview of the important data points for all your products and listings, and you can make the basic adjustments on inventory manually. These adjustments include revising prices, quantity changes, tracking your shipment at every stage, adding new products to your inventory, and even viewing who the other sellers of the same product are. You'll be able to track this data on a monthly and weekly basis. You could even do it daily if you wanted to, and it helps you keep track of the trending patterns you see. Getting a comprehensive look at your inventory data is how you make informed purchasing decisions.

Your stock is going to go through what is known as an "inventory turnover rate." To figure out what your rate is, you need to know how quickly your products sell on average on Amazon. With this information on hand, you will be able to gauge how much stock you need to keep your stock levels healthy in between your inventory shipments. If you want to prevent overbuying or under-buying, this is the way you do it. Generally, what Amazon sellers would do would be to import goods based on a three-month turnover rate. What this means is for the stock that you order, you can expect to sell out within that three-month period. Another way to predict how quickly your turnover rate is going to be is by using a tool to help you forecast and track the number of sales you make daily. This tool is also available as part of Amazon's inventory forecasting options under the Amazon Selling Coach. You will be able to track your sales based on your available stock, and the two will help you recommend the quantities you need to fill orders over a specified time frame.

As a new seller, Amazon's inventory management tool is going to be your best asset. Use it, in the beginning, to quickly and seamlessly manage your larger inventories and update your information as you go. Continuously track how your inventory is performing. You will find all the useful information that you need to help you sell better under this option, so be sure to use it to your advantage. A lot of new sellers make the mistake of underutilizing this tool.

Best Tools to Help You Manage Your Inventory

Sellers on Amazon have different needs when it comes to inventory. A seller moving a few products have different preferences compared to sellers who are multichannel and need to stock and reorder products in bigger volumes. If you wanted to explore other options to help you manage your inventory, these are some alternatives to the Amazon FBA option:

- Joelister - Assuming that you're operating on eBay and Amazon FBA, Joelister is how you would easily and quickly fulfill and list your Amazon inventory on the eBay platform. This option offers sellers a one-click solution that will automatically populate all your eBay listings complete with product info and description. It also syncs the quantities of your items between eBay and Amazon and automates the fulfillment process. Once you've sold an item on eBay and the payment has been successfully processed and received, Joelister passes the order along to Amazon to handle the shipping. As a bonus, this third-party management tool even helps you upload your tracking numbers and send them to eBay.

- Brightpearl - This option helps you manage your orders, inventory, finances, and your customers all within one single system. The biggest benefit for sellers who are using this system would be the efficiency involved and the insight that they get to help them accelerate both their profits and their growth. This is done through multi-channel retailing, both online and offline, accounting, and order management software. Brightpearl even office sellers the added convenience of integrating with other third-party systems, including the likes of Amazon, eBay promo, and Shopify to make it even more convenient.

- Restock Pro - Save time tracking your shipments and your inventory with this cloud-based management tool that could help you accelerate your business. Whether you are manually trying to fulfill orders from your own warehouse, or you're a seller on FBA, this platform lets you track of your vital data related to inventory, help you streamline your operations, forecast your sales, manage your suppliers, create custom kits, and even print custom stickers.

- Skubana - Another cloud-based management tool is Skubana, and it has helped many entrepreneurs build a successful multi-channel E-Commerce business. With the 1-Click integration it offers for Amazon, eBay, shopping carts, and other marketplaces, sellers get to leverage Skubana's business intelligence and power. There is a catch, though. You need to be bringing in at least 1,000 orders monthly to do this. The platform believes that anything less than this specific number of orders means you're wasting your time and selling more means you are radically operating at unprecedented levels.

- Seller Active - This multi-channel listing manager offers sellers the convenience of efficiently helping you maximize your E-Commerce product reach. Boost your presence across numerous marketplace dominators like Amazon, Walmart, and eBay. Other perks of this platform include being able to consolidate your orders for easy packing, shipment, and tracking. Seller Active uses helpful alerts and accurate reporting for real-time visibility into your orders, listings, and sales. Basically, you never have to worry about going out of stock or overselling. Sellers get to easily and conveniently build a centralized product catalog for themselves and the convenience of their customers. You could upload your new listings in bulk across multiple channels and resolve any specific marketplace issues within a faster timeframe.

- TradeGecko - As a powerful cloud-based platform that serves small and medium businesses, as well as business-to-business wholesalers, TradeGecko provides sellers with a multi-channel inventory and complete order management system. The experience you get with this option is highly personalized, and it is one of the best platforms out there that gives you options like order and inventory management, integrations and operations, analytics, reporting, and more.

Shipping Your Inventory to Amazon

After you have chosen the supplier that you want to work with, and you have received the samples that you ordered from them, you will then need to work on shipping those items over to Amazon's fulfillment centers. To do that, you will need to create a shipping order before you can proceed. This can be done easily on the Amazon Seller Dashboard on your profile. Here's what you need to do step-by-step:

Step 1: Log in to your Seller Account and go to the "Inventory" tab. This should be available on your dashboard.

Step 2: Under this tab, select the "Manage FBA Inventory."

Step 3: Select the checkbox located on the left of your product. Click on this checkbox, and then select "Action on one selected."

Step 4: When you've done that, select the "Send/Replenish Inventory" option.

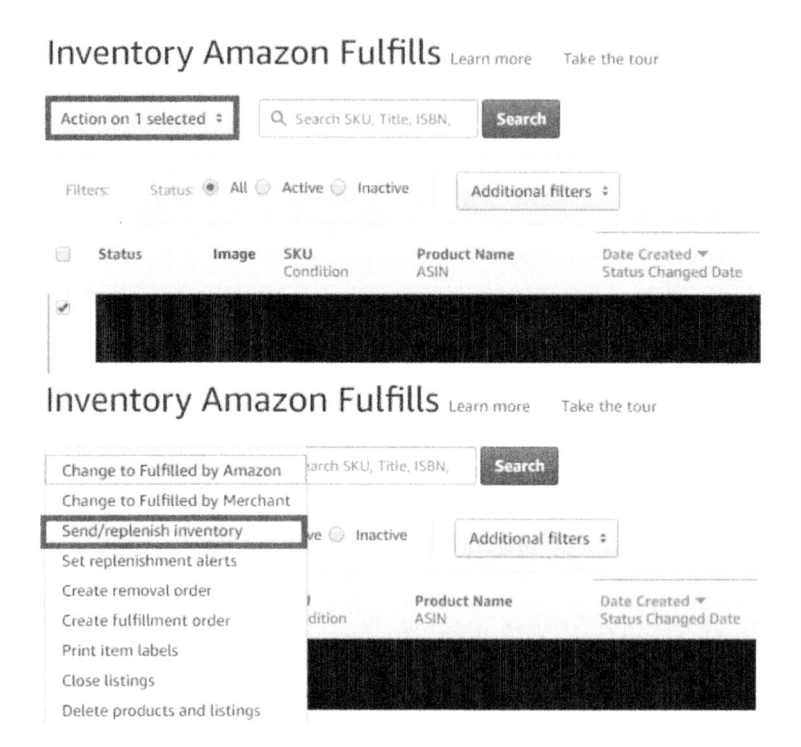

Image Source: Thomas F. Adams

Step 5: After you've done that (this is on the assumption that your products are FBA listings), the next thing you need to select is "Send Inventory". Amazon will prompt you to do it if you've already converted to an FBA merchant account.

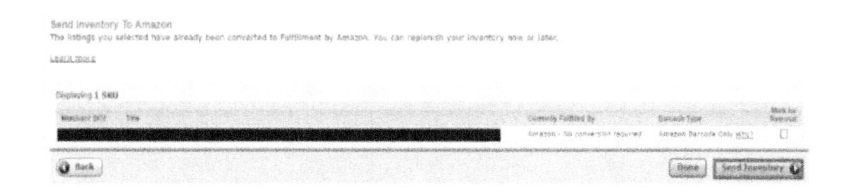

Image Source: Thomas F. Adams

Step 6: Scroll down when you arrive at the next screen. You'll see a part where you will need to key in the number of units and cases you'll be shipping. If you're sending 10 sample items in one box, select "10" in the "Units per case" box. Under "Number of cases," choose one box. Fill out the details and

click "Continue."

Image Source: Thomas F. Adams

Step 7: The next part involves preparing your products. Each product must be sent to Amazon in an individual polybag complete with its own warning label. If you're getting your products from a supplier based in China, you should already receive the items in polybags.

> **Warning:** To avoid danger of suffocation, keep this plastic bag away from babies and children. Do not use in cribs, beds, carriages or playpens. The thin film may cling to nose and mouth and prevent breathing. This bag is not a toy.
>
> **Advertencia:** Para evitar peligro de asfixia mantenga esta bolsa de plastico fuera del alcance de bebes y ninos. No lo use en cunas, camas, carriolas o corralito para bebes. La capa fina de la bolsa se puede pegar a la nariz o boca y puede impedir la respiracion. Esta bolsa no es un juguete.
>
> **Attention:** Garder ce sac hors de portee des bebes et enfants. Ne pas utiliser dans les berceaux, lits, poussettes ou parcs a bebe. Le film protecteur, etant fin, pourrait par inadvertance provoquer l'etouffement en bloquant les narines ou/et la bouche. Ce sachet

Image Source: Thomas F. Adams

Why Private Labeling Matters

Private labeling has grown in popularity in recent years. You might have even come across this term as you were doing your research about going into the FBA business. A lot of online retailers these days are going the private labeling root for their products. Why they are choosing this option is because private labeling gives your product a unique identity. Additionally, it showcases your brand as a seller. In terms of marketing your products, private labeling is the better option to choose if you are looking to build a strong reputation for your brand in the long-run. How does private labeling work? It's simple. The first thing you would need to do is buy the products you want from your chosen supplier. You will then sell it under your brand name. The conventional way of running a business would be manufacturing the products yourself. But that is not how it works in this case. You won't be manufacturing your products. Instead, what you will do is to create a private brand, and then put all the products that you bought from the supplier under that brand. You will then resell them on your Amazon FBA platform.

Filling The FBA Inventory

In general, Amazon sellers are so focused on finding new products on Amazon that they often forget to maximize the profitability of their existing product package.

It's easier to increase your company's profits through proper inventory management than doing research on new products. Effective inventory management ensures that you do not miss any products that you want to sell when customers want to buy and that your money is properly invested in the right products so you can transfer your inventory to earn profits.

Below is a discussion with Jeremy Biron, founder of Forecastly, the main difficulties that Amazon sellers face in restocking FBA, including supply chain management and stockpile prevention.

Question: Why did you decide to create an inventory management tool?

My experience is e-commerce and internet marketing, with a particular interest in the Amazon market. We created the internal software about 3 years ago. We wanted to do the FBA refill correctly.

I've seen what kind of software is available on the market, and when I completed warehouse management training, I also found major shortcomings in the management of FBA inventories in terms of restructuring and inventory levels.

That's why I chose Forecastly about a year ago, after receiving the same comments from other Amazon providers. Shortly thereafter, we had our first sellers on the platform.

Q. What are the biggest challenges in replenishing FBA inventories?

1) Calculation of the sales speed:

Many of the seller's problems (at the time the company was founded) concerned the wrong calculation of sales speed. Since then, some applications have resolved this issue, which is a good thing - but it was an integral part of our decision to start the business.

If a product is out of stock or unavailable for half a month and you sell 100 units, the situation is very different if you sell 100 units and the product is in stock because your sales speed should be double that. she was.

If you do not correct this at the beginning of the process, the other failed calculations that you perform after that moment are irrelevant. This is the beginning of the refilling process. If this is not the case, then everything that will follow is flawed after that time.

2) Integrate the turnaround time:

Another important element of inventory management is the precise integration of deadlines. For a large number of applications, deadlines are not adequately taken into account - this is the time of stocks.

Assuming that your processing time is 30 days and 45 days, you are very likely to have a stock of 15 days, which can be very expensive for a seller.

According to Forecastly, "vendors often underestimate the impact of an out-of-date FBA on an Amazon company, and you obviously run out of product sales if you do not have stock in stock, which is the most obvious problem, but you do not have to stock the impact of an event is to take into account your inventory forecasts in the future. "

"Sellers often underestimate their forecasts when an item has recently sold out, a problem that amplifies when the Out of Stock event has occurred over an extended period of time.

 3) Anticipate top sales:

The other challenge is to accurately predict the likelihood of revenue growth. If you can predict a peak, you can probably reduce the risk of shortages.

An increase in sales could include external factors such as promotions and seasonality. These are two elements that are difficult to integrate into your forecasts and that you cannot easily identify in an Excel spreadsheet (where many salespeople calculate their stock levels).

Excel works very well if you are a small seller. However, if you want to do it properly on a large scale, you need to be able to accurately predict those peaks and include those external factors in your forecasts.

This is mainly due to the seasonality of the Amazon, which refers to the category level for a certain period of the year. Sellers should also be aware of the impact of advertising. For example, if you give 100 units at a 50% discount because you want to stimulate the sale, you cannot assume that the sales speed of 100 units will persist after you stop giving units at 50%.

Inventory management is about a lot of "secret sauce". You do not have to know exactly how this works, but as a seller, you need to know what's included in your equation, including seasonality and / or promotions. The same sold out for days. It's important to know what the system does, but not necessarily how it does it.

It is very important that sellers ask themselves if they think it pays to send their suppliers and their costs directly to Amazon.

I do not think the Amazon refill tool works as well as some other tools available on the market, though at the same time, it may also be beneficial for some smaller vendors - a starting point.

1. You cannot just rely on Amazon

Although Amazon FBA provides you with some inventory management tools, it is assumed that you have a stock of your self-stored products. However, as more and more vendors use Amazon FBA or other alternative execution methods, such as the purchase of dropshipping, this is becoming increasingly rare. Even then, Amazon will notify you (at the most) a few weeks later, and there is not always enough time to refill.

How can you be proactive in this regard? By knowing your sales speed and delivery cycle. The easiest way to do that is by not just relying on the tools provided by Amazon. If you invest in FBA management software, rather than relying on the Amazon-powered dashboard, you can set up your own resupply notifications and keep your inventory up-to-date. This will ensure that you do not disappoint your customers with overdue orders or excessive sales.

2. Pay attention to every product

All your products are unique - and you have to treat them that way. It's easy to consolidate orders and save costs and shipping costs. However, this will not benefit you if half of your inventory stays on the shelves and does not sell like the other half. This means that you have to examine each product individually and order the stocks accordingly. Of course, the best artists have to be reorganized more frequently, while your slow actions should only be bought when they move.

It can be beneficial to automate the sales cycles of some of your products once you have an idea of their performance. Make sure that you also take into account the latest trends and the current situation: Seasonal sales waves can have a big impact on how much inventory you need.

3. Keep an eye on your promotions

Actions are a great way to increase sales, generate ratings, and improve your ranking on Amazon. But you have to monitor them.

Of course, you want your promotions to work well. However, if they work too well, serious inventory issues can occur. If they are too successful, it can significantly reduce your profit margins (much more than expected). The worst case is the unexpected failure. In that case, all the work you have done with promotion to improve your rankings was useless. Not only will you lose potential sales, but you will also reduce your ranking and have an additional deficit in the beginning.

To counter unsuccessful promotions, you can create a protected inventory from your inventory in the Seller Central part of Amazon by placing an order for yourself. You can keep the inventory for two weeks. So, if you find that your promotion is starting and your inventory is low, you can stop the action and cancel the order as this inventory is automatically offered for sale.

4. If you have concerns, keep an extra reserve

You may have heard of Just-in-Time Inventory Management, which does not keep inventory but only orders for sale. This approach is ideal for controlling inventory and reducing costs. But for Amazon salespeople, keeping stock levels that way while keeping customers satisfied is very difficult. You need to closely monitor your inventory and know the exact periods of increased demand.

For this reason, it makes sense to reserve part of your budget to provide additional reserve when needed. This can be done through additional products that keep you ready, cost your inventory, or reserve extra space in your warehouse. Emergency Planning helps you prepare for when things are not going as planned - what you need to sell successfully on Amazon.

Need more advice from Amazon? Here are common mistakes to avoid in Amazon inventory and tips for reducing long-term storage costs for Amazon FBA.

Whether you're new to the Amazon market or a seasoned salesman, you're certainly making mistakes along the way. Some manufacturer errors can cost time and money, while others prohibit selling to Amazon, such as the wrong inventory management on Amazon.

Common Errors that Sellers make

The ten most common errors committed by Amazon sellers are the following. Try to avoid them at all costs.

1. Wrong prices and stock quantities

The lists and quantities available on Amazon are put online almost immediately. New sellers have no opportunity to practice before. Make sure you list your inventory carefully. If you have no inventory, enter zero. If you have stocks, specify the quantity exactly.

It is also important that your prices are listed correctly. It happened that sellers accidentally came in for a very low price and that their products sold quickly, which cost them thousands of dollars. Using Amazon Inventory Automatic Inventory Sync Software is the best way to manage Amazon Inventory Management.

2. Descriptions of elements that do not match

Amazon makes it easy to match existing product lists with the product you sell. Do not forget to be very careful when doing this. You need to make sure your ad portrays exactly what you sell. If your customers receive products that are almost identical to those in your ad, they can complain and you can be suspended if your ad does not match the right product.

3. Ignore policy changes

If you receive an email or other notification that Amazon has changed a policy, do not search it and press the Delete key. It is essential that you read it vigorously and check that the changes are correct for you. Reading takes only a few minutes, and most changes are minor. As a result, compliance usually does not take long. This can prevent you from being paused or terminated.

4. No clear return policy

It is inevitable that a customer wants to return a product at a certain time. It is important that you clearly specify your return policy so buyers can be informed and make an informed decision before purchasing. You do not want to interact with your customers, resulting in a complaint or negative feedback.

5. Do not collect comments

Amazon's Supplier Performance and Product Quality department oversees seller feedback for each sale, quality (rank), and quantity (typically receiving about 5 percent of sales feedback). If you are low in one category or another, your account may be suspended. You may want to think about a vendor who will assist you in applying for feedback - there are several, including Feedback Genius and FeedbackFive.

6. Does not respond quickly to customers

When an Amazon customer sends you a request, you have 24 hours to respond, whether it's a weekend or a public holiday. If you do not respond to the customer's request within the given time, you will be notified by Amazon. If this happens too often, your account may be suspended. Respond quickly to requests for information, even if the request or problem cannot be resolved immediately.

7. Performance error

If you are a new salesman and execute your own order, it is easy to make mistakes. Maybe the delivery of an order has been delayed a bit. You may forget to share tracking information with Amazon, or you may feel that you are no longer up-to-date and need to cancel an order.

It is important that you master your order from the beginning. You may want to consider the Fulfillment by Amazon program if you are considering automated transfers or both.

8. Do not use the right tools

As an Amazon seller, you just cannot do it all by yourself. There are various tools you can adopt to make your business smoother. Do not try to do everything yourself. Find the right tools to help you.

9. Competing against Amazon

Before purchasing or listing an inventory on Amazon, check whether Amazon Retail sells the products. The fight against Amazon Retail is likely to be a losing battle as it manages its capability to win the sale, sometimes even at a loss. You can check Keepa to see if the product you want to sell is already on Amazon Retail and list it accordingly.

10. Be contented

It can be easy to stop checking on and analyzing your company's status and indicators, especially if everything is alright. However, as it often takes some time for differences to occur, it is important to stay informed, even if your business is successful. This helps you to take advantage of trends and edit areas that need to be improved long before they become a problem.

Inventory Management Amazon requires a lot of experimentation: see what works and what does not, then make adjustments. However, if you know some of the common mistakes, you can avoid major disasters. To understand Amazon's inventory management, you need to stay up-to-date, sell quality products, provide great customer service, and get to know your business.

Fulfillment By Amazon (FBA) suppliers may not be aware of Amazon's long-term FBA storage fees for products that have been placed on Amazon shelves for more than a year.

According to Amazon, products that are either stored or stored too long in their warehouses limit the ability to make room for fast-selling, low-cost products.

For example, Amazon cleans up inventory on the 15th of each month and rates the so-called "long-term storage costs" for its BAF customers whose inventories were stored too long in their data centers. Commands.

How much does FBA long-term storage cost from Amazon?

It depends on what you have in stock. Amazon charges you the highest of two scenarios:

In space: $ 6.90 per cubic foot for inventories stored for more than 12 months

Per unit: $ 0.15 per storage unit stored for more than 12 months.

Depending on what you sell, Amazon will calculate your costs based on the two scenarios above and charge you the highest amount.

Yes, it's a bit hard to understand. For example, suppose you sell small key chains and have about 100 in an FBA warehouse. You may not need much space, say a cubic foot. If you do not sell these key fobs and store them on the Amazon shelves for 365 days, Amazon will charge your fees:

Per room: $ 6.90, as your key fobs occupy one cubic foot of their warehouse.

Per unit: $ 15, as you have 100 key fobs, each costing $ 0.15.

Amazon will charge you $ 15, as this is the highest value.

How to avoid long-term storage costs

Now is a great time to consider what you can do to avoid Amazon's long-term FBA storage costs.

- Check the status of your inventory

The first step is to determine the status of your inventory and determine if you might have to pay a fee. If you have FBA inventory management software, such as: For example, the solution offered by Ecomdash allows you to generate reports and use calculator tools that tell you what you need to know. Otherwise, you can access the Amazon Inventory Health status report to see if any inventory was stored too long in Amazon distribution centers.

- Determine how risk assets should be managed

Once you identify the vulnerable inventory, you must propose a strategy to avoid long-term storage costs. You have a few options:

- Request the distance

It's the easiest option. If you submit a removal request, Amazon will return your requested inventory to your company for a small fee. The return shipping cost can be up to $ 0.50 per unit, oversized products only $ 0.60 per unit. This may be the most trustworthy way to avoid long-term storage costs as long as you can afford to meet your margins.

- Application for removal

Your second option is to file a cancellation request. For a price that is below the payout price, Amazon keeps the stock for you. Choosing this option can be difficult. However, if the amount you have paid for your inventory is minimal, it may be the best. Maybe you've tested a new product that has not sold, so it's time to cut the bait.

Unfortunately, you will be charged a fee even if you choose Amazon for your inventory. The exclusion is $ 0.15 for standard size units and $ 0.30 for oversized units. The good thing about the elimination is that Amazon makes things easier. All you have to do is choose to remove the products and Amazon will do the rest.

Avoiding Common Mistakes

You now have the information required to start your FBA business and become successful. While you will become a perpetual student and researcher in your path to growing your business, you've started off on the right foot. To wrap up everything, I want to dive into a few things we haven't covered.

There are a handful of very common mistakes often made by new entrepreneurs working with Fulfillment by Amazon. This list is not comprehensive, but these are some of the most dangerous things to your bottom line that you can easily avoid. It can save you a lot of time that would be wasted on researching and implementation as well.

Dropshipping

Dropshipping is the process of working with a manufacturer or supplier that ships items on your behalf. While this method of e-commerce is viable, there is not a lot of room for it when utilizing Fulfillment by Amazon. Having your supplier ship to Amazon for you may sound like a great idea, but unless they are willing to label your products as required by Amazon for FBA sales, you'll be paying Amazon 0.20 cents per label. Additionally, this takes out the step of checking your products for quality, and if you're not handling your own shipments, many things can go wrong. Amazon requires you to follow their specifications, and your dropshipping supplier is going to charge you whether they do this correctly or not.

In most dropshipping situations, you're only looking for a supplier to ship one item at a time to customers rather than amounts that you can justify with FBA businesses. If you want to work with a dropshipper, there's no reason to handle this through FBA at all. You can list items that aren't fulfilled by Amazon and process them one at a time instead. This can be a great way to earn money that has very little risk involved, but the profit margins aren't always going to be as high per sale since products aren't as cheap as buying wholesale.

Price Wars

Do not engage in pricing wars, and do not try to always undercut the lowest seller. This does nothing but drives down prices, and in the end, everybody except the manufacturer and supplier just makes less money. Because you'll be using FBA and qualify for Prime shipping to your customers, you don't even need to price the lowest price to make your sales anyway. Do not engage in pricing wars; you're just hurting yourself.

Shady Reviews

Do not, in any situation, try to pay money to have fake Amazon reviews added to your private label products or any listing you've created on your own. This is usually easy to spot by Amazon, and even when they miss it, your customers often feel cheated once they purchase a product if it doesn't meet the expectations created by fake reviews. If you need more reviews, then you need to offer your product to people in exchange for reviews. Tell them that they can be upfront that they were given the product to review, and tell them that you're looking for honest reviews. If you are taking your time to ensure you provide high-quality products, you should be garnering good reviews anyway. If you have a number of bad reviews, take their criticism into consideration and fix the problems.

Losing Money When Buying Overpriced Products

If you have somehow made the mistake of paying too much for a product, there are a number of options you have to attempt to make a small profit or at least avoid a loss. This includes:

- If it is an item bought from a larger supplier or a retail operation, they may actually accept returns. You may have to pay a restocking fee or at the very least return shipping, but it is better than sitting on a product you cannot make a profit on anyway.
- Sell through other means. If you can make a little bit of profit by shipping these products yourself, considering selling them outside of the FBA program and simply handling orders on

Amazon yourself for this particular item. Likewise, you can use eBay or other marketplaces to sell these products as well. If selling online simply isn't going to be worth the loss, then you might attempt to sell them in bulk to someone else locally or online just to get rid of them. You may be able to get your money back or very close to it, but even if there's a loss, at least it won't be as horrible as simply losing all the money you put into the investment.

- Use the item as a free giveaway, contest, or other marketing ploys. This works especially well for those items that are branded for private label sales, as you're likely marketing with the use of social media and/or a website anyway and actually have a reason to have a free giveaway in order to hopefully drum up additional business.

- Bundle with other products to create a new product listing with added value. If there is any hope of bundling this product with another product that makes sense, you may even be able to make your money back and some profit. In the worst-case scenario, losses will be minimized since you're not spending extra to ship or sell the product.

- Keep in mind that you can write off your losses. While this won't really translate to making your money back, it will translate to paying less in taxes.

At the end of the day, it is unlikely that every product is going to be a huge earner. There is always some risk involved, and this is especially true when working on products that aren't available on Amazon already or attempting to brand your own products for private label sales.

Avoid the End of a Trend

One huge mistake people make is that they are far too late to the game on a trend. Catching a trend before it blows up can be a quick way to make a huge chunk of money, but if you're coming in at the tail-end of a trend and the market has already by oversaturated with copycat sellers, then you may find yourself sitting on a product that's far too available in the market to really turn a profit. The time to join in on trending items is at the first whiff of their popularity, not after the market becomes so flooded that prices are quickly dropping. This is especially true of products that practically any manufacturer can make, as there will quickly become a ton of cheap options available.

Not Taking Risks Is the Worst Mistake You Can Make

While this chapter is all about avoiding risk, one of the biggest risks any entrepreneur can ever make is not taking any risks whatsoever. You want to make calculated risks. Taking risks is what leads to huge payouts. A surefire product will probably sell well, but your profit is going to be very expected as well. You have to be willing to take a chance sometimes.

Let's think back to trending items. Who do you think most likely made the most money on these products during the height of their popularity? It was the people that jumped on the train before it was completely viral and saturated by less adventurous sellers. They were able to foresee a product blowing up. They couldn't completely prove that this would be the case, but the trends showed that it could happen. Some items will start to blow up and fizzle out almost immediately, and most of us understand that as sellers, but rather than wait around to find out, they jumped on and took the risk.

Don't take this advice wrong, though. If your capital is limited, you need to work on products that are going to make your profit with some certainty. You need to grow your capital enough that taking a risk and failing isn't going to end your adventure. To limit the personal damage that risk-taking can have on your finances, don't forget that registering your new enterprise as its business entity can help protect your personal assets. If your business goes bankrupt, you won't lose everything. But if you're making sure to have the capital ahead of taking very large risks, any hiccups should be recoverable down the road.

Just being an FBA seller is taking a risk to begin with, though, and that first leap into your financial freedom is an act of bravery. You believed in yourself, and you should!

Conclusion

Now that you have made it to the end of this book, you hopefully have an understanding of how to get started creating your own passive income stream with FBA, as well as a strategy or two, or three, that you are anxious to try for the first time. Before you go ahead and start giving it your all, however, it is important that you have realistic expectations as to the level of success you should expect in the near future.

While it is perfectly true that some people experience serious success right out of the gate, it is an unfortunate fact of life that they are the exception rather than the rule. What this means is that you should expect to experience something of a learning curve, especially when you are first figuring out what works for you. This is perfectly normal, however, and if you persevere you will come out the other side better because of it.

The next step is to stop reading and to start doing whatever is required of you to ensure that yourself and those you care about will be on good financial grounds and stability. If you find that you still need help getting started you will likely have better results by creating a schedule that you hope to follow including personal milestones and practical applications for various parts of the tasks as well as the overall process of acquiring the life-changing knowledge and experiences.

In this light, studies show that complex tasks that are broken down into individual pieces, including individual targets, have a much greater chance of being completed when compared to something that has a general need of being completed but no real time table for doing so. Even though it would seem silly, go ahead and set your own deadlines for completion, complete with indicators of success and failure. After you have successfully completed all of your required milestones, you will be glad you took that former step

Once you have finished the initial process it is important to understand that it is just that, only part of a larger plan of preparation. Your best chances for overall success will come by taking the time to learn as many vital skills as possible. Only by using your prepared status as a springboard to greater profit margins will you be able to truly rest soundly knowing that you are finally taking the right steps into realizing your financial balance and stability, not to mention prosperity.

Printed in Great Britain
by Amazon